Exploring
The Smokies

Published by Great Smoky Mountains Natural History Association, a
private, nonprofit organization supporting the national parks since 1953.

Edited by Stan Canter, Don DeFoe, Steve Kemp, and Diane West
Coordination and production by Steve Kemp
Design by Lee Riddell
Printing by Adams Lithographing Company

To purchase additional copies of this book, please write:
Great Smoky Mountains Natural History Association
115 Park Headquarters Road
Gatlinburg, Tennessee 37738

Front Cover. A colorful forest floor. ADAM JONES.
Back Cover. Rose Houk. MICHAEL COLLIER.
P.5 Blue ridges. JOHN NETHERTON.
P.6 Morton Overlook near Newfound Gap. HOWARD KELLEY.
P.7 Bloodroot. JOHN NETHERTON.
P.10 Smokies footbridge. HOWARD KELLEY.
P.11 Violet. JOHN NETHERTON.
P.42 Cades Cove. FRANCIS DORRIS.
P.43 Columbine. JOHN NETHERTON.

ISBN 0-937207-03-9

Wood-sorrell, with its candy-striped flowers and shamrock shaped leaves, thrives in the Smokies' high elevation forests.

JOHN NETHERTON.

acknowledgments

Thanks to the Great Smoky Mountains Natural History Association for the opportunity to write this book and a chance to return to the wonderful Appalachian Mountains. Above all, the Association's publications specialist, Steve Kemp, deserves credit for acting as editor, organizer, advisor, and friend. The Association's executive director, Diane West, was a great help as well. Stan Canter, long-time chief of interpretation at Great Smoky Mountains National Park, was always there when I needed him. Other Park Service people, especially Glenn Cardwell, Don DeFoe, Pam Boaze, Elden Wanrow, Ed Trout, Robert Wightman, Margie Steigerwald, and Tom Robbins answered endless questions, offered excellent advice, and provided crucial logistical assistance. Much gratitude goes to Annette Evans, whose indispensable knowledge guided me to the right resources in the Park library, and to Ken Voorhis, who extended gracious hospitality from the Smoky Mountains Institute at Tremont.

I must also acknowledge, however inadequately, all the unnamed people who wrote the newspaper articles, guidebooks, and other specialized publications that were essential to the background research for this book. Thanks to all the fine people of the southern mountains, whose warm hearts made me feel at home, and to my family, who was always there, eager to support me all the way. Thank you all. 🍁

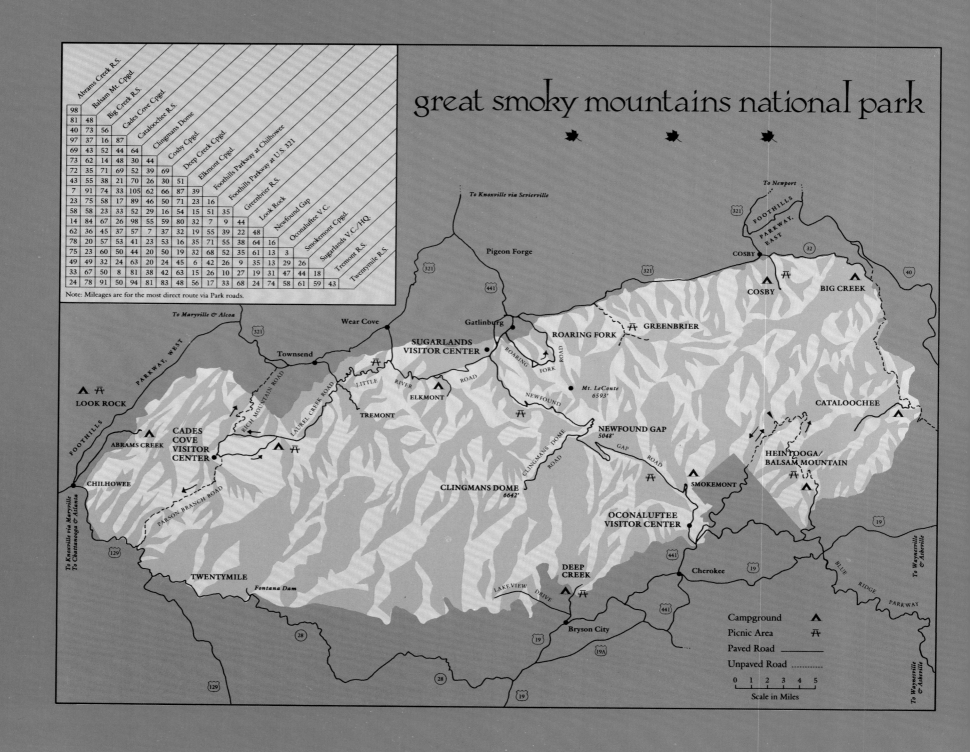

contents

travel planner

You won't find any billboards or amusement parks at the remote Wear Cove entrance to the Park. HOWARD KELLEY.

travel planner

To get a head start on your trip to Great Smoky Mountains National Park, contact Superintendent, Great Smoky Mountains National Park, Gatlinburg, TN 37738, telephone (615) 436-1200. The Park is within 600 miles of two-thirds of the population of the United States, and receives nine to ten million visits a year. Certain times, especially the summer months, weekends in October, and holidays are periods of heaviest visitation. During these times accommodations and campgrounds are often filled early in the day, and traffic congestion is common in the more popular areas.

Getting Here

Towns and cities closest to the Park served by air are Knoxville and Chattanooga, Tennessee; Asheville, North Carolina; and Greenville, South Carolina. Atlanta, Georgia, also has air connections but is a five-hour drive from the Park.

The Park is accessible primarily by private automobile, from Interstates 40 and 75.

No commercial bus or train service is available to the Park. Tour bus excursions may be arranged through travel agents.

Where To Start

Great Smoky Mountains National Park has three staffed visitor centers where you can become oriented, have questions answered, and purchase books and maps about the Park. Sugarlands Visitor Center is two miles south of Gatlinburg, Tennessee; Oconaluftee Visitor Center is three miles from Cherokee, North Carolina; and Cades Cove Visitor Center is located in the Cable Mill area of Cades Cove, fifteen miles from Townsend, Tennessee.

Supplies

There are no grocery stores or camping supply stores in the Park, except for the small camp store at Cades Cove. See Accommodations for nearest town where supplies may be purchased. THERE ARE NO GASOLINE STATIONS IN THE PARK.

Weather

Spring weather, especially in March, is unpredictable, with sunny skies and snow possible on the same day. Summer is hot and humid, with afternoon showers common, and temperatures in the 80s and 90s. September through mid-November are drier months, with warm days in the 70s and 80s and cool nights. Freezing temperatures at night are expected in October. Winter is moderate, but heavy snowfalls can occur at high elevations in January and February.

Elevation in the Park ranges from 800 to 6,642 feet, thus the weather changes simply by going up or down the mountains. Be prepared with suitable clothing at all times of year.

For current weather conditions call (615) 436-1200 in Tennessee; (704) 497-9146 in North Carolina.

Camping

Ten National Park Service campgrounds are maintained in the Park, suitable for tents and recreational vehicles. Three are run on a reservation system, and reservations are needed in the busy summer months, and October as well. None have electrical, water, or sewer hookups. The daily status of campground vacancies can be obtained at the visitor centers. Many private campgrounds are located outside the Park, and showers and laundries are also available nearby. (See the Camping section on page 45 for further information.)

Handicapped Accessibility

Sugarlands, Cades Cove, and Oconaluftee visitor centers and the Cable Mill area at Cades Cove are accessible to wheelchairs, and designated parking spaces are located close to the buildings. Restrooms at the Cades Cove, Sugarlands, and Oconaluftee visitor centers are also accessible. Trails at the Oconaluftee Pioneer Farmstead are hard-packed gravel and are wheelchair accessible with assistance. Reservations for a "handicapped campsite" at Cades Cove, Elkmont, and Smokemont campgrounds can be made through the reservation system. These, along with Cosby, Big Creek, Cataloochee, and Abrams Creek campgrounds, have accessible restrooms. Recorded tapes, printed materials, and temporary parking permits are also available at Park visitor centers. A leaflet listing all accessible facilities in the Park is also available.

Accommodations

Lodging and eating establishments are extremely limited in the Park. Gatlinburg, Pigeon Forge, and Townsend, Tennessee, and Cherokee, North Carolina, are the closest surrounding towns with accommodations. Information can be obtained through the following chambers of commerce:

NORTH CAROLINA
  ▷ Bryson City Chamber of Commerce
    P.O. Box 509
    Bryson City, NC 28713
  ▷ Cherokee Tribal Travel and Promotion
    P.O. Box 460
    Cherokee, NC 28719
  ▷ Jackson County Chamber of Commerce
    18 N. Central Street
    Sylva, NC 28779
  ▷ Maggie Valley Tourist Bureau
    P.O. Box 87
    Maggie, NC 28751

TENNESSEE
  ▷ Gatlinburg Chamber of Commerce
    P.O. Box 527
    Gatlinburg, TN 37738
  ▷ Maryville Chamber of Commerce
    309 S. Washington
    Maryville, TN 37801
  ▷ Sevierville Chamber of Commerce
    866 Winfield Dunn Parkway
    Sevierville, TN 37862
  ▷ Pigeon Forge Department of Tourism
    P.O. Box 1390
    Pigeon Forge, TN 37868
  ▷ Townsend Information Center
    7906 E. Lamar Alexander Parkway
    Townsend, TN 37882

destinations

DRIVING DISTANCE FROM
(in miles)

Gatlinburg 27
Cherokee 57
Townsend 9

FACILITIES
Campground
Amphitheater
Restrooms
Store (closed in winter)
Bicycle rentals (closed in winter)
Horse rentals (closed in winter)
Picnic area
Visitor Center with exhibits and
*   sales area (open April-October)*
Ranger station
Frontcountry horse camp
Backcountry permits

HIGHLIGHTS
Eleven-mile, paved loop road around the cove with self-guiding auto tour booklet, restored historic buildings, working grist mill, wildlife viewing, hiking trails, special events and demonstrations of mountain crafts, Parson Branch and Rich Mountain backroads.

cades cove

Cades Cove is in several ways a window. Historically, the cove is a place that lets us look in on a way of life now gone. Biologically, the meadows and forests harbor native wildlife, and a visit to the cove allows us to observe them in their natural land. And geologically, the cove exists as a "window" of limestone revealed by erosion.

As outsiders looking through the window, we can learn much about pioneer life in the Smoky Mountains. Cades Cove contains one of the most complete collections of restored historic structures in the Southern Appalachians. Along the eleven-mile loop drive around the cove we can visit the places where the first settlers were born and grew up, where they labored, where they worshiped, and where they died.

These early settlers followed the Indians into this low mountain cove. In fact, the name Cades Cove is believed by many to be a corruption of the name Kate, the wife of Cherokee chief Abram. By 1821 the wave of migration had begun; most people entered from Virginia and North Carolina, seeking one of the most precious commodities in the mountains —

flat land for farming. The Tiptons had the first recorded legal land title for Cades Cove, and not far behind were the Olivers, Cables, Shields, Gregorys, and Anthonys.

Cades Cove experienced steady population growth during the early years of settlement. In 1830, the census showed 271 inhabitants in 44 households; in 1840, 451 people in 70 households; and by 1850, a peak of 685 living in 132 households. In ensuing years the population fluctuated, but averaged about 500 people.

The pioneers, like those everywhere in the new country, had to furnish their basic necessities of food, shelter, and clothing. They created "new ground" in the forest by girdling trees to make them die. A circular cut was made through the bark that interrupted the flow of water and nutrients, so that the tree eventually died in place and fell to the ground. In these clearings, or "deadenings" as they were called, the ubiquitous field of corn was planted. The men set about hewing the straight poplar trees into flat-sided logs for houses and barns and corncribs. The women gathered ramps in the spring, berries in summer, and chestnuts in fall, and their gardens were planted in beans, peas, and potatoes. They cooked on woodstoves, and spun the yarn and wove the cloth to make their clothes.

Because they had little cash to spend, early Cades Cove residents could barter at Russell Burchfield's store for those goods they couldn't make or find on their own. Coffee, tobacco, cough syrup, castor oil, suspenders, nails, lard, lye, and "enbordry" thread could be paid for in peas, chickens, eggs, corn, or ginseng.

A big occasion for mountain people was a visit to the local mill on milling day. John P. Cable's water-powered grist mill, built in the 1880s, still grinds away and is a popular attraction in Cades Cove. Cable joined the waters of Forge and Mill creeks by canal, dammed up a pond, and opened a gate to bring the water through the millrace and into the wooden flume.

The water from the flume pours over a reconstructed wooden water wheel which turns the heavy grinding stone inside the mill. You can feel the soft cornmeal pouring warm from the spout into the cloth bag, and today's miller will kindly tell you all you want to know about the operation, including when the freshest meal went up to the visitor center for sale.

John's daughter Becky, known to most everyone as "Aunt Becky," lived in the large frame house that now sits beside the mill. Part of the house was originally a store, which Aunt Becky helped manage, along with her other duties of farming, livestock herding, keeping boarders, spinning, weaving,

The unpaved Rich Mountain Road offers this view of Cades Cove and the Methodist Church (left). JOHN NETHERTON.

You can still see corn being ground at the Cable Mill in Cades Cove (right). JOHN NETHERTON.

The John Oliver place is typical of a mid-nineteenth century home on the eastern frontier. FRANCES DORRIS.

cooking, and caring for her brother's orphaned children.

Undoubtedly, the residents of Cades Cove knew times both of plenty and of want. But no matter what the state of prosperity, they always found time to thank their Lord. They gathered in the neat white churches—invariably Baptist or Methodist—and sang the familiar hymns and caught up on the latest gossip. The children probably squirmed on the hard benches, just as they would today, and counted the seconds until they could bolt for a cool swim in the creek. D.B. Lawson gave half an acre and helped build the Methodist Church in Cades Cove. And to assure that it never fell into secular hands, he deeded the land to "God Almighty."

Cades Cove is a window in yet another way. Geologists call it a "fenster," the German word for

window. In the upheavals that occurred during creation of the Appalachian Mountains, older rock got thrust over younger. In Cades Cove that sheet of older rock has since eroded to form a break or "window" that exposes an underlying younger limestone.

Limestone-based soils are hospitable to the grasses that carpet the idyllic meadows of Cades Cove, and contribute to a stream quality that trout find inviting. The fields are still being grazed and farmed to maintain the open character of settlement times. At the edges, where field meets forest, wildlife can often be seen, especially in early morning and late afternoon. Animals that once would have meant food on the table are now protected from hunting. Commonly a herd of white-tailed deer is seen munching the soft grass, posing nicely for the throngs that photograph them from their car windows. And wild turkey can be spotted occasionally in the meadows.

The animal that creates the biggest hubbub is the Smokies trademark, the black bear, cause of a phenomenon called a "bear jam." When one is sighted, cars stop in the middle of the road, and drivers temporarily abandon their vehicles to snap pictures of the bear. If you're caught in the gnarl, you might think you were in rush-hour Manhattan instead.

Fascination with the bears is understandable, for they are magnificent animals; and the Smoky Mountains are one of the few places in the eastern United States where they can be seen in their own habitat, doing what they naturally do. The important thing to keep in mind at Cades Cove and elsewhere in the Park is that they are *wild* creatures, not pets.

If the traffic jams begin to remind you of what you had hoped to leave behind on your vacation, simply park the car and set out afoot to see the cove. Amble into one of the spacious meadows, spread out a blanket, and picnic far from the madding crowds. Or walk up the half-mile, self-guiding Cades Cove Nature Trail, as fine a place as there is in the mountains

for exploring a diverse hardwood forest. Abrams Falls is a five-mile roundtrip hike off the loop road, ending at an eighteen-foot-high waterfall. From the picnic area, a twelve-mile loop trail, part of it on the Appalachian Trail, leads to Spence and Russell fields where the pioneers once grazed cattle.

Worthwhile backroad adventures await you on a couple of one-way gravel roads accessible from the Cades Cove loop road. From your vehicle you can experience more gently the trip that the settlers made by wagon over the Rich Mountain Road. This one-way winding route offers high views of Cades Cove, and you may also see wildlife along its twelve miles to Townsend, Tennessee. Or you may travel the Parson Branch Road, which tracks deep into the forest and through heavy rhododendron stands for eight miles

before it ends at Highway 129 on the southwest edge of the Park. Both roads are closed in winter. Both are passable to regular passenger vehicles, but large campers and buses should not attempt them.

Cades Cove is the kind of place that brings people back, time and again. Upon each return, you will see more of what made this place home to early pioneers. If you're here at the right times of year, you may see sorghum molasses being made, hear stories being told, or learn about old quilts. Each time, and each new experience, makes that view through the Cades Cove window a little clearer. ❧

Mornings and evenings are especially good times to spot deer and other wildlife in the cove (left). JOHN NETHERTON.

Hyatt Lane is a quiet backroad which offers a shortcut across Cades Cove (right). HOWARD KELLEY.

DESTINATIONS
16

DRIVING DISTANCE FROM
(in miles)
Gatlinburg   60
Cherokee   39
Townsend   81

FACILITIES
Campground
Ranger and information station
Restrooms
Frontcountry horse camp
Backcountry permits

HIGHLIGHTS
Auto tour of cove and historic structures with self-guiding booklet, hiking trails, fishing, horseback riding, Cataloochee Creek.

cataloochee

The bell tolled twenty-nine times, once for each name read from the list. Someone's father, brother, mother, son or daughter—a somber litany of those who had passed away since homecoming a year ago.

All heads were bowed in Palmer Chapel on this sultry August Sunday. But as the people mourned the deaths of friends and neighbors, they also celebrated those who were still able to attend this gathering.

"If I see the sixth of November, I'll be ninety-one years old," said one man, who stood in response to the question of who was the oldest person present. He was soon outdistanced, however, by a blushing woman who rose and quietly announced that she was ninety-four.

Cataloochee Homecoming. Once a year on a Sunday in August they come back to the valley where they were born and raised, arriving now in cars and trucks and RVs instead of on horseback or in wagons—the Palmers, Woodys, Caldwells, and Hannahs, among others. They park on the newly mowed lawn and walk up, greeting people they haven't

seen for a year and asking newcomers, "And what line are you from?" If you admit to being a stranger, you won't be one for long. For the people of Cataloochee—in typically hospitable mountain style— will sweep you into the fold without a moment's hesitation. Gradually they filter into the refurbished chapel, white as starched linen, where it's standing room only. The congregation sings with abandon the old hymns, "Amazing Grace" and "What a Friend We Have in Jesus."

They or their ancestors all once lived here in this beautiful cove—until 1934 when the National Park Service bought their land. Upon first hearing of the rumors of the buyout, the people of Cataloochee were astounded. Some left willingly; others held out as long as they could.

It's easy to see how hard it would be to leave Cataloochee. For this remote mountain valley on the eastern edge of the Smoky Mountains casts an undeniable spell over nearly everyone who has been here. "What is it about Cataloochee?" I asked a friend who ranks it among his favorite places in the world. Without hesitation he answered, "It's perfect." Many share his sentiment. Some say Cataloochee is a Cades Cove without all the people. The eleven-mile gravel road into Cataloochee seems to sift out those

uninterested in making the effort to reach this isolated spot.

Beyond sheer beauty, perhaps the stong, deep sense of the history of this place attracts people here. The Cherokee first named it *Gadalutsi,* which means "standing up in a row" or "wave upon wave." They may have been referring to the rows of trees on the peaks or the swells of blue mountains stretching to infinity. They were the first who entered, following the trails of the buffalo. And a few found a hiding place here in 1838 when the rest of their tribe was driven along the tragic Trail of Tears to Oklahoma. Cataloochee also served as a hideout for "Outliers," Civil War protesters who did not wish to choose sides in the conflict.

Others, attracted by the bounty of game and fish and rich bottomland, came to spend their lives here. Henry Caldwell made a land entry in 1814, but most arrived over the Cataloochee Trail a little later—in the 1830s and 1840s. Not all these settlers were Scotch-Irish, as is commonly thought. Elizabeth Powers has written that there were French, English, and "a regular distillation of German, Irish, Welsh, and Scotch . . . making quite a heady brew."

Childhoods spent in Catalooch, as it's affectionately called, were halcyon days. "They was raspberries and strawberries and June apples and all sorts of fruit, and it was more like livin' in the Garden of Eden than anything I can think of," recalled one man of his boyhood there.

But the children may not have realized all the fears and responsibilities that adulthood can bring. Cataloochee was wild country. One oft-repeated tale is of two neighbor women who kept fires burning in the fireplaces all night to stop the screaming panthers from coming down their chimneys. Men protected the community from outside attack and engaged in back-breaking labor to build the Cataloochee Turnpike, the toll road that connected them to the outside world.

Part of Cataloochee's "spell" is the way human history and wilderness surroundings blend together (far left). FRANCES DORRIS.

Palmer Chapel is the site of the Cataloochee homecoming, where families and friends return to decorate graves, attend services, and enjoy one of America's most delicious potluck dinners (left). HOWARD KELLEY.

Cataloochee offers many miles of horse trails, but you'll have to bring your own steed (right). NATIONAL PARK SERVICE.

In Cataloochee a man's reputation was made or broken by his prowess as a bear hunter. One man became a legend in his own time. "Turkey George" Palmer claimed to have killed more than a hundred bears in his life. Many remember "Turkey George" as a short muscular man, most often seen walking alongside his horse, Old Sank, and carrying his knapsack on his chest. He hunted alone without using dogs.

"Turkey George" got his name, they say, when as a young boy he tried to catch some turkeys with bait in a log pen. The trap worked, but when George went in the pen to capture one, the turkeys "mighty nigh" killed him, he said.

You can walk to the place where this famous pen was built—from the Beech Grove School it's a pleasant hike along Palmer Creek on the trail of the same name. In about a mile and a half, the Pretty Hollow Trail bears right to the backcountry horsecamp now located at "Turkey George's" old home place.

Other hiking opportunities in Cataloochee include walks to some magnificent old trees. Cataloochee was not as ravaged by logging as were other parts of the Smokies, and awe-inspiring hemlocks and white pines still stand along the Boogerman Trail, off the Caldwell Fork Trail near the campground. (The trail generally follows a road built by hand by Robert Palmer, who earned the nickname Boogerman as a youngster. When the teacher called on him, he was so shy he hid his head on his desk and simply muttered "Boogerman.") Fourteen footbridges span Caldwell Fork, and one is the longest in the Park. About five miles up the Caldwell Fork Trail, an unmarked side trail leads down to virgin yellow-poplars, one of which takes seven men with hands joined to embrace its circumference.

Besides hiking and horseback riding, fishing is a popular pastime. Many a campfire tale has been told regarding the infamous "One That Got Away." But once in a great while an angler will produce hard proof—a photograph of an impressive twelve-pound

brown trout—attesting to the fact that Cataloochee Creek does contain some whoppers.

Next to Cades Cove, Cataloochee holds the best collection of restored homes and buildings in the Park. A self-guiding auto tour booklet available at the beginning of the paved road will explain the history of both Big and Little Cataloochee. Will Messer's Barn, Palmer Chapel, Beech Grove School, and the Caldwell, Woody, and Palmer houses are among the structures you may visit.

You might want to spend a fall morning just sitting on the steps of the footbridge that leads to Hiram Caldwell's large blue and white frame house. Frost crystals line the grasses, softly backlit by a welcome morning sun. As the sun climbs higher in the sky, the frost quickly melts and steamy vapors rise off the fields. Horseback riders pass, huddled on their saddles and blowing into cupped hands. A few visitors stop to take pictures. But beware the spell of Cataloochee. It comes on without warning and is difficult, if not impossible, to lose. ❧

The edges of Cataloochee's meadows are good places to look for deer, bear, wild turkey, and other wildlife (far left). FRANCES DORRIS.

Hiram Caldwell's new house, with its weather boarding and shiny Sears & Roebuck paint, was the talk of the valley when it was completed in 1906 (left). HOWARD KELLEY.

Flowers of the yellow poplar tree are filled with rich nectar that bees love (right). FRANCES DORRIS.

DESTINATIONS
20

DRIVING DISTANCE FROM
(in miles)
Gatlinburg   22
Cherokee   25
Townsend   40

FACILITIES
Observation tower
Restrooms

HIGHLIGHTS
Three-hundred-sixty-degree view from highest peak in the Park, paved trail to observation tower, hiking trails to balds with azalea and rhododendron blooming in early summer.

clingmans dome

A mountain woman once said, "A little height makes a sight of difference in the way a body sees things." She could well have made the comment after coming down from the top of Clingmans Dome.

In the vernacular of the Southern Appalachians, a dome is a high peak. At 6,642 feet above sea level, Clingmans is *the* highest peak in Great Smoky Mountains National Park, and as such hundreds of thousands of people come to see it each year.

In the old days the spur road to Clingmans Dome used to be called the Skyway. You certainly feel like you're in the heavens as the road follows the top of old Smoky for seven miles, hugging the boundary line between Tennessee and North Carolina. Views that can only be described as majestic await the traveler around nearly every curve.

Originally called Smoky Dome, the peak was renamed by nineteenth-century geographer Arnold Guyot, in honor of General Thomas Lanier Clingman. A U.S. Senator and Confederate brigadier general, Clingman had climbed and measured the peak in 1858, and later had a trail cleared from Indian Gap to the point so Guyot could remeasure it. For some years Clingman and Professor Elisha Mitchell had engaged in a disagreement over which mountain was actually higher—Clingmans Dome or Mount Mitchell in the North Carolina Blue Ridge. Professor Mitchell eventually won (Mount Mitchell is 6,684 feet), but he didn't live to savor his victory. In 1857, while exploring his namesake mountain, he fell to his death.

A half-mile paved trail leads from the parking area to the observation tower on Clingmans summit. A 375-foot ramp with a 12 percent grade spirals up to the lookout, forty-five feet above the ground. (Some people turn around and walk backward up the ramp to ease the strain on their calf muscles.) Signs describe the geography you may see on a clear day from the tower. On a foggy day, of which there are many up here at these heights, you may have more trouble picking out the landmarks. But the fog often comes and goes; if you stay awhile the heavens may open to reveal those mind-boggling, eye-stretching vistas.

Up here it rains a lot. Ninety inches a year, give or take a few. That much moisture at this altitude translates to a forest more like that of the Far North of this continent. On the way to Clingmans Dome you pass through a cool, dark forest of red spruce and Fraser fir. You may wish to stop on the way back to Newfound Gap and take a walk on the self-guiding Spruce-Fir Nature Trail to become better acquainted with this fascinating—and rare—forest of the southern mountains. Seven "islands" of spruce-fir forest have been identified on the crest of the Southern Appalachians, isolated vestiges of the last ice age. They harbor animals and plants unique to the region: seven subspecies of birds and some forty-five species of plants occur only in these spruce-fir islands.

And it is often cold in these mountains. One April day, though the sun was shining when we left Sugarlands, ice coated the needles of the trees up at Clingmans Dome. The wind reminded us that we had returned to winter. A jacket, and even hat and gloves,

On a good day it seems like you can see all the way to heaven from Clingmans Dome (far left). FRANCES DORRIS.

The ½-mile trail to Clingmans Dome is an interesting place to explore the Park's rare spruce-fir forests (above). FRANCES DORRIS.

can be welcome at any time of year. In winter the road to Clingmans Dome is closed. Snowfall is great enough to warrant leaving the road unplowed for the pleasure of cross-country skiers. All this rain and snow contribute to the making of the Little River. The stream's headwaters are on Clingmans Dome, whence it tumbles nearly a vertical mile to the flatlands near Elkmont, out to Maryville, and eventually into the mother river, the Tennessee.

From the Clingmans Dome parking area, hiking trails present good opportunities for entering the Smokies backcountry. Two balds are accessible—Andrews Bald, only two miles on the Forney Ridge Trail, or Silers Bald, four miles west on the Appalachian Trail. 🍂

Here it is, the
TOP TEN LINEUP
of the Highest Peaks
in the Great Smokies,
for those who can't resist playing
"Which One Is Highest?"

1. Clingmans Dome	6,642'
2. Mount Guyot	6,621'
3. Mount LeConte	6,593'
High Top	6,593'
4. Cliff Top	6,555'
5. Mount Buckley	6,500'
Mount Love	6,500'
Myrtle Point	6,500'
6. Mount Chapman	6,430'
7. Old Black	6,358'
8. Blazed Balsam	6,243'
9. Luftee Knob	6,216'
10. Mount Collins	6,188'

SOURCE: *Decisions of the United States Geographic Board, Number 28.* June 30, 1932. United States Government Printing Office.

The Clingmans Dome observation tower is the highest point in the Smokies (sidebar). HOWARD KELLEY.

DESTINATIONS
22

DRIVING DISTANCE FROM
(in miles)
Gatlinburg   *21*
Cherokee   *54*
Townsend   *42*

FACILITIES
Campground
Amphitheater
Ranger station
Picnic area
Restrooms
Horse rental
Backcountry permits

HIGHLIGHTS
Waterfalls, trails, less visited.

cosby

Cosby has at least one thing going for it: the picnic tables have moss growing on them. What that means to you and me is that this is still a relatively unvisited area, by Smokies standards.

When all the other campgrounds in the Park are bursting at the seams in midsummer, Cosby will have a few vacant sites—and no reservations required! In spring, when flocks of people are ogling wildflowers on popular trails, the Cosby Nature Trail is largely untraveled.

It's only another half-hour drive east from Gatlinburg to get here, but for some reason Cosby remains undiscovered. Perhaps part of the explanation rests in its reputation. Tucked away in the northeast corner of Tennessee, Cosby has always seemed to hold secrets.

For a long time Cosby's claim to fame was as the "Moonshine Capital of the World," especially during the depression, which also happened to be the early years of parkhood. Cosby was part of warden Audley Whaley's beat in those days, and he testified to the abundance of stills and their products in the area.

When he found one in the Park, he would leave a note ordering removal or the still would be destroyed. Though his job demanded that he enforce the law, Whaley said that many moonshiners had to engage in their trade to feed their families.

An event that has put Cosby on the map—in a more favorable light—is the annual Ramp Festival sponsored by the local Ruritan Club. Now if you've never tasted a ramp, you don't know what you're missing. These wild leeks, described as a cross between an onion and garlic, can "make Democrats smell like Republicans and Republicans smell like Democrats," quipped one lawyer. The festival, held on a Sunday in April, has been attended by thousands over the last thirty years. The appearance of Tennessee Ernie Ford in 1957 marked the biggest year the festival has ever known. The delicacy of the day, of course, is ramps, fried with some fatback bacon, with a piece of cornbread on the side. So if you're thinking of changing your political party, dig in.

Any other time of year, though, Cosby offers quiet camping and peaceful picnicking. Once you're here, you may wish to investigate further because there's more to do than meets the eye. Hiking trails, from the shady stroll along the nature trail to the challenging steepness of Snake Den, await all comers. The Appalachian Trail is readily accessible, only two and a half miles up Cosby Creek Trail. The four-mile roundtrip to Henwallow Falls makes a perfect dayhike. You may also ride a horse, visit a pioneer cemetery, or attend a campfire program in the amphitheater.

In summer you may find a special treat, a sunset walk to Sutton Ridge with a ranger. One August evening I joined Ranger Tom Barnes and several families, flashlights in hand, for this hike. As we started up the trail, Ranger Tom pointed out the pencil-straight trees that surrounded us. These are yellow-poplars, trees that have grown in since the forest was logged in pre-Park days, and which prevail at lower elevations all over the Smokies. Along the trail we noticed patches of ragged ground that looked as though something had been digging there—recently. Indeed, advised Tom, these scratchings were the handiwork of hungry black bears pawing through yellowjacket nests for larvae. Unavoidably, from that moment on every dark stump and rustling in the woods became a bear, just waiting for twilight hikers.

In a mile and a half we reached the overlook on Sutton Ridge, named for a family of settlers in Cosby. The sun was a giant red watermelon veiled by the ever-present Smokies' haze. Tom pulled out topo maps and we tried to get our bearings. We lingered and savored the view, heading back just as the sun sank below the mountaintops. On the way down, darkness closed in around us. A twelve-year-old and I told ghost stories. An owl called in the woods. We watched for bears. Cosby. Thank goodness for its secrets. 🍂

There are worse things to do on a hot afternoon than to dip your feet in a cool, clear mountain stream near Cosby Campground (left). JOHN NETHERTON.

The cemeteries near Cosby reveal the effects a hard life in the mountains had on infant mortality and life expectancy (right). HOWARD KELLEY.

DRIVING DISTANCE FROM
(in miles)
Gatlinburg   47
Cherokee   15
Townsend   65

FACILITIES
Campground
Ranger station
Amphitheater
Sheltered picnic area
Restrooms
Backcountry permits

HIGHLIGHTS
Short hikes to waterfalls, hiking trails, fishing, tubing.

deep creek

The Cherokee Indians have a story about how *Shaconage,* the Smoky Mountains, were modeled. At one time the earth was soft and wet and flat. Great Buzzard flew over the land, and when his wings wearied they struck the mud and thus the valleys were formed. On each upbeat of his wings a mountain was raised.

The Great Smoky Mountains were the heart of the Cherokee domain. Their once-extensive empire covered parts of eight states, including western North Carolina and almost all of Tennessee and Kentucky.

Cherokee society was organized into seven clans—Wolf, Blue, Paint, Bird, Deer, Long Hair, and Wild Potato—and each had a chief and "mother town." One of the mother towns, Kituwha, may have been located near the present Deep Creek Campground. The Cherokee developed a written alphabet based on syllables in their language, and in 1828 the first edition of the *Cherokee Phoenix,* a newspaper in Cherokee and English, was released.

Despite these notable achievements, ten years later the tragic end of this highly developed, thousand-year-old society was assured by the United States government. In 1838, 15,000 Cherokees were herded at rifle and bayonet point to follow what became known as the Trail of Tears to Oklahoma. Four thousand died along the way. Cherokee farmer Tsali, with a small band, took refuge in a rock shelter at the head of Deep Creek, to avoid being captured. But a year later Tsali, his brother, and his son were executed by a firing squad. The remnant group that managed to survive and stay in the homeland would form the Qualla Reservation, just south of Great Smoky Mountains National Park.

Meanwhile, whites had come to settle on Deep Creek, among them Abraham Wiggins, along with the Shulers and the Millsaps. They planted crops, fished the waters of Deep Creek, and worked on the railroads and in the sawmills that came into their county in the 1880s. Like their Tennessee neighbors, they too faced removal when the national park was formed in 1934.

Now Deep Creek is a place for recreationists. In summer the creek is wall-to-wall tubers; people of all ages careen down the stream in black inner tubes and then walk back up the road for another spin. They pitch their tents in the campsites near the creek for easy access, while those who seek a quieter camping experience choose the higher loops of the campground.

Three lovely waterfalls are within easy dayhiking distance of the campground. Tom's Branch Falls is a short walk up Deep Creek, though its threads of water are partly obscured by tree branches. About three-fourths of a mile farther up the trail is Indian Creek Falls, on a tributary of Deep Creek. This is a good place to sit and watch yellow swallowtails play in the mist of the rushing water. Up another side creek from the parking area is Juneywhank Falls, where in only a half-mile stroll you may have the entire place to yourself, even on the busiest summer day. A ranger at Deep Creek gave me a rough translation

of Juneywhank—in Cherokee it means "place where the bear passes."

An eight-mile hike up the Deep Creek Trail will take you to a historic spot of sorts, the last permanent campsite of Horace Kephart. A librarian by profession, Kephart in 1903 left his family and a good job in St. Louis to live a life of solitude deep in the Smoky Mountains of western North Carolina. Home was an abandoned miner's cabin on the Little Fork of the Sugar Fork of Hazel Creek, with the "mysterious beckoning hinterland . . . right back of my chimney," in Kephart's words. Fascinated by the mountaineers, their originality and customs, and their skill as woodsmen, Kephart wrote a classic study, still in print, entitled *Our Southern Highlanders.*

In 1909 he moved to the small village of Bryson City at the mouth of Deep Creek. Before his death in 1931, Kephart worked tirelessly to see that his beloved Smokies became a national park. It was Bryson Place, up Deep Creek, where he would set up camp, sometimes for an entire summer. A local Boy Scout troop erected a plaque there, commemorating the place where "Horace Kephart—dean of American Campers and one of the principal founders of the Great Smoky Mountains National Park—pitched his last permanent camp." 🍂

Tom's Branch Falls is just a ¼-mile stroll up the Deep Creek Trail (far left). JOHN NETHERTON.

Water is always in a hurry in the Smokies, where over 600 miles of streams rush down the mountainsides, but there are no natural lakes or ponds (left). JOHN NETHERTON.

Indian Creek Falls is an easy two-mile roundtrip hike on the Deep Creek Trail (right). HOWARD KELLEY.

DRIVING DISTANCE FROM
(in miles)
Gatlinburg   6
Cherokee   39
Townsend   28

FACILITIES
Picnic areas (sheltered and open)
Ranger station
Backcountry permits

HIGHLIGHTS
Early homesites, hiking trails, Middle Prong of Little Pigeon River, fishing, swimming.

greenbrier

If Glenn Cardwell had the time, he would probably like personally to escort every visitor to the Smokies through Greenbrier Cove. Glenn, a ranger with the National Park Service, grew up in Greenbrier and stories of the place bubble from him like water from a "bold" spring.

There's a cranefly orchid, at least that's what Glenn's mother called it. She taught him all the names of the plants and their uses, and consequently he is a walking encyclopedia of botany. And there's the Huskey cemetery, and yes, he says, the graves do face

east because mountain people believed that on the Second Resurrection Christ will come from the direction of the rising sun. This is the old garden spot, where Glenn's father dug sweet potatoes, and here's the picnic area, once "Blacksmith John's Place," and the "Baptizing Hole," where Glenn recalls that they had to crack the ice in the stream before the service could take place.

The wildness of Greenbrier today hides the fact that this was once one of the most populated communities in these mountains. The center of the

community was where the store, post office, school, and church were located. Glenn can still see the folks sitting out on the porch of the country store, a "place of utility . . . where you could go and have your teeth pulled, get your hair shingled, or make bets."

The covered picnic site was a former Civilian Conservation Corps camp where Glenn's brother lived and where Greenbrier homecomings now are held. When the former residents return, they still bring jugs to fill with the clean water from the spring here.

Greenbrier is a day-use area, and in addition to the old homesites and cemeteries, it offers the gorgeous Middle Prong of the Little Pigeon River for fishing or swimming. Hiking is another good possibility. One of the more popular ones is the hike to Ramsay Cascades, an eight-mile roundtrip to the highest waterfall in the Park. Another fine hiking trail is located at the head of Greenbrier Cove along Porters Creek. For a mile it is an easy walk along an old

jeep trail. Then a split occurs, with one trail going up to Brushy Mountain and the other continuing up Porters Creek. Glenn recommends Porters Flat in spring as one of the most beautiful wildflower spots in the Park. About a mile-and-a-half up Porters Creek is Fittified Spring, a name given by mountain folk because it was "spasmodic," ebbing and flowing.

Water was what caused people to settle in one place, Glenn believes. If a good "bold" spring was located, that was home. To this day mountain people attribute good health and longevity to the water. It made them as strong and tough as the tenacious greenbrier vine that has taken over all the old home places. When the Park Service bought their land and the people of Greenbrier had to leave their homes, besides saying goodbye to friends and neighbors one of the hardest things they had to do was leave that pure water. 🍁

June visitors to the Smoky Mountains are treated to one of the finest displays of rhododendron found anywhere (far left). FRANCES DORRIS.

Greenbrier is a hub for hiking trails leading to waterfalls, the Appalachian Trail, Mt. LeConte, and destinations throughout the Park (left). HOWARD KELLEY.

Hikers who make the eight-mile roundtrip hike to Ramsay Cascades are rewarded with one of the most spectacular waterfalls in the Park (right). HOWARD KELLEY.

DESTINATIONS
28

DRIVING DISTANCE FROM
(in miles)

Gatlinburg	51
Cherokee	20
Townsend	69

FACILITIES
Campground
Picnic area
Restrooms
Ranger station
Backcountry permits

HIGHLIGHTS
Heintooga Overlook, beginning of Round Bottom Road, hiking trails, high country.

heintooga – balsam mountain

Balsam Mountain. April 20. A mile above sea level and the trees have not yet leafed out. Down in the valleys the hillsides are an infinite variety of greens, and the dogwood, serviceberry, and redbud are in full bloom. But up here spring is still several weeks away, and the only flowers brave enough to open their buds are the candy-striped spring beauties. They had bloomed almost a month earlier in the lower elevations, and are a pleasant reminder that coming to the high country of the Smokies is like following spring north from Georgia to Maine.

The road up Balsam Mountain features fantastic views north to the main crest of the Smoky Mountains, with sixteen peaks attaining elevations of 6,000 feet or more. Until mid-May a gate across the road blocks the last few miles to Heintooga Overlook and Balsam Mountain Campground. From mid-May through mid-October the campground, tucked on the top of Balsam Mountain at 5,310 feet, is a respite from the heavy, monochromatic green that cloaks the low country. Balsam Campground is also an excellent base for more extensive exploration of the area.

You may start with the Balsam Mountain Nature Trail, accessible from the campground, but be forewarned: "the use of this trail could be habit-forming and beneficial to your health." To cope with this high-elevation experience, bring camera or sketchbook, hand lens, and binoculars. As you walk, listen and watch for black-capped chickadees, veeries, and juncos, "snowbirds" that inhabit this northern hardwoods forest in summer but retreat to lower elevations in winter.

A highlight of a visit to Balsam Mountain is a drive on the Round Bottom Road, one of those Smokies backroads visited by only a handful of people. It's a good gravel road, thirteen miles one-way through a beech and yellow birch forest and down into the hardwoods. It then becomes a two-way gravel road for five miles, then nine more miles of pavement along Raven Fork back to Cherokee, Oconaluftee Visitor Center, and the Blue Ridge Parkway. The Round Bottom Road is closed in winter and is not suitable for large vehicles. The road provides access to several trailheads, including Spruce Mountain, Palmer Creek, Balsam Mountain, Beech Gap, and Hyatt Ridge trails.

Heintooga Overlook, at the picnic area near Balsam Campground, offers the evening's entertainment. Sunset seen from this point is one of those "peak" experiences of a trip to the Smokies. Delicate peach, orange, and yellow-tinted clouds streak the sky in silent progression as night inches up over the massif of the mountains. In autumn the same colors, with splendid splashes of crimson, are reflected in the leaves of the trees. As I watch, an obvious though no less remarkable revelation occurs to me—just as spring moved up the mountain, autumn moves down the mountain in the endless cycle of the seasons, as certain as change itself. ✦

The mile-high Balsam Mountain area offers splendid views of the Great Smoky and Blue Ridge Mountains (left). FRANCES DORRIS.

Fall begins on Balsam Mountain when summer is still in full swing in the valleys below (right). FRANCES DORRIS.

DESTINATIONS
29

DRIVING DISTANCE FROM
(in miles)

Gatlinburg	*37*
Cherokee	*65*
Townsend	*18*

FACILITIES
Campground
Picnic area
Restrooms
Backcountry permits

HIGHLIGHTS
Views of the Smokies from outside Park, hard-surfaced trail to observation tower and exhibits.

look rock

Look Rock was the place to be for fashionable gentlemen and ladies of the nineteenth century. When they tired of billiards and croquet, they came up from the spacious Seven Gables Hotel, a popular spa at Montvale Springs that was billed as "The Saratoga of the South" during its heyday.

On nice afternoons they would follow a three-mile trail to have a look from the rock on top of Chilhowee Mountain. As early as 1832 the sight was declared to "comprise one of the best views in the United States." The trip became an Easter Sunday tradition that lasted into the middle of this century.

In keeping with this well-earned fame, Look Rock now features an observation tower, accessible by a half-mile, hard-surfaced trail off the west end of the Foothills Parkway. From this relatively high point (about 2,700 feet elevation) the view *is* exceptionally interesting, especially for the contrast. To the east hulk the ramparts of the main Smokies, while to the west lie the flatlands of the Tennessee Valley, the town of Maryville, and the Cumberland Mountains in the distance.

The Look Rock area is an off-the-beaten-path destination with plenty of views and elbow room (left). FRANCES DORRIS.

Look Rock offers camping, picnicking, an impressive observation tower, and cool evening breezes (right). FRANCES DORRIS.

Long, slender, Chilhowee Mountain is interesting geologically because it is one of the few places in the Smokies with rocks of Paleozoic age. Specifically, these rocks are sandstones and limestones laid down about 500 to 600 million years ago. They are old rocks, but not as old as those that form the core of the Smokies, which date back beyond 900 million years. In this dim time in the geologic past the Ocoee Series, as it is named, was also laid down as sedimentary rock. But through application of heat and pressure—and unfathomable time—these sedimentary rocks were changed, or metamorphosed, into the gneisses and schists and slates that outcrop along most roads and trails in the Park.

Look Rock Campground is located across the road from the observation tower. It is a delightful summer outpost in a less crowded atmosphere where cool breezes almost always blow. The open dates of the campground vary from year to year, but it is usually only open during June, July, and August. 🍁

DESTINATIONS

32

DRIVING DISTANCE FROM
(in miles)

Gatlinburg 15
Cherokee 17
Townsend 33

FACILITIES
Restrooms
Parking area

HIGHLIGHTS
View of Park, interpretive waysides, access to Appalachian Trail.

newfound gap

President Roosevelt was late. The crowd of 25,000 people, including all the dignitaries that could possibly be assembled, waited at Newfound Gap on Labor Day, 1940. Franklin Delano Roosevelt was to dedicate Great Smoky Mountains National Park, but his party was forty-five minutes behind schedule.

He finally arrived, and after the minister delivered a lengthy invocation, FDR officially dedicated the eastern United States' largest remaining wilderness as a national park. "For the permanent enjoyment of the people" reads the inscription on the bronze plaque at Newfound Gap, with an expression of gratitude to those who made this Park a reality.

The story of the creation of Great Smoky Mountains National Park is long and complicated. Basically, the Park's existence is owed to some far-sighted, dedicated individuals who would not give up in the face of the immense task that lay before them. The 500,000 acres of the Park rest in two states, Tennessee and North Carolina, all of it then in private ownership. More than 6,000 individual parcels had to be acquired, through a painful and expensive process—both to obtain the money to buy the land and to remove people from their homes.

By the time negotiations were complete, money had run short. John D. Rockefeller, Jr., through his mother's foundation, the Laura Spelman Rockefeller Memorial, gave five million dollars to match the amount contributed by the two state governments. When word of the Rockefeller donation was heard in Knoxville, bells and whistles went off in celebration.

Newfound Gap thus has earned a significant place in the history of the Great Smokies. It is now a destination for a large percentage of visitors to the Park. Originally, a place called Indian Gap, about two miles west of Newfound, was the point at which two toll wagon roads met to cross the mountain barrier. But a "newfound" gap, or pass, proved to be slightly lower and so became the pass through which the transmountain road would go.

The road, completed in 1932, is a treat in itself. There are pullouts, wayside exhibits, and picnic areas along the way, and a dramatic change in forest types occurs during the 3,600-foot ascent. At Newfound Gap you can straddle the line between North Carolina and Tennessee, learn from the exhibits, and feast your eyes on the spectacular views from this high point. The seven-mile spur road to Clingmans Dome also joins at Newfound Gap.

The Appalachian Trail crosses the road here, nearly halfway on its seventy-mile route through the Smokies. Well-muscled, heavily laden backpackers seem in a hurry to be back on the dirt path, rather than in the midst of a parking lot. Others use this point as convenient access to begin a hike either east or west on the "AT." A popular hike to Mount LeConte heads east on the AT to the Boulevard Trail; another favorite destination along this same route is a point called Charlie's Bunion, with sheer 1,000-foot dropoffs and what some insist is the most inspiring view in the Park. ❧

5,048-foot Newfound Gap was the easiest route engineers could find for crossing the mountains between Tennessee and North Carolina (far left). JOHN NETHERTON.

Wayside exhibits at Newfound Gap delve into Park history, wildlife, and some threats to the area (above). HOWARD KELLEY.

You may encounter some heavily-laden hikers at Newfound Gap, the point where the 2,000-mile-long Appalachian Trail crosses the main Park road (left). HOWARD KELLEY.

DESTINATIONS
34

DRIVING DISTANCE FROM
(in miles)

Gatlinburg   31
Cherokee   1
Townsend   47

FACILITIES
Visitor Center with orientation
Sales area
Exhibits
Restrooms
Ranger station
Backcountry permits

HIGHLIGHTS
Working pioneer farmstead with self-guiding booklet, living history demonstrations and special events, working grist mill, access to Blue Ridge Parkway.

oconaluftee

Folks from around these parts pretty much recognize all the produce that grows in Tom Robbins' garden. "Those sweet potatoes?" they ask. "Yes they are," Robbins replies. Free samples of purple hull peas fresh from the pod are passed around and receive nods of appreciation.

Dressed in bib overalls and black hat, Robbins tends not only to the garden but to the other unending chores at the Pioneer Farmstead at Oconaluftee. He has a master's degree in Appalachian Studies, but has plenty of dirt under his fingernails too. To Robbins,

his job with the Park Service is not so much a demonstration as real life—the way the early settlers lived it. The Pioneer Farmstead is more than a romantic re-creation. It is intended to duplicate as authentically as possible the small family farm, the basic economic unit of frontier America.

One noteworthy crop in the garden is the corn, which even in a drought-ridden summer towers fifteen feet above the ground. People know it's corn, but many may not recognize the variety. It is Hickory Cane, a white field corn that dates at least to 1850.

It is still available through places that specialize in old seeds, and seems to do fine in the rich bottomland soil of the Oconaluftee River valley.

Besides the garden, the Pioneer Farmstead presents an impressive collection of original log buildings—the Davis house, Floyd barn, and Jim Beard's corncrib among them—and it is well-fixed with ducks, geese, cows, horses, hogs, and a rooster that has the run of the barnyard. Butter and milk chill in the springhouse, the hog is ready to butcher, and honey has just been harvested from the beegums. The self-guiding brochure to the farmstead tells more about the buildings, the people, and how they fed, clothed, and sheltered themselves here in this river valley.

Oconaluftee, or "Luftee" as it is familiarly known, was once home to the Cherokee, and the word in their language means "by the river." Rising in the high mountains just below Newfound Gap, the Oconaluftee River flows for twenty-three miles, half that length coursing through what is now Great Smoky Mountains National Park. Its "beautiful and fertile though narrow flat bottoms" were admired by geographer and explorer Arnold Guyot.

The fertile land, unquestionably flat by Appalachian Mountain standards, has been long and well-used. Seven archeological sites have been identified in the Oconaluftee area, from 8,000 years old to historic Cherokee times. As early as the 1790s white settlers began to arrive in this part of North Carolina. The John Jacob Mingus family was the first to stay permanently, with Ralph Hughes and Abraham Enloe, followed by the Sherills, Conners, Collins, and Carvers. Like their contemporaries in places like Cades Cove, these farmers grew corn and raised cattle. The Oconaluftee Turnpike, built by the residents and finished in 1839, provided access to markets on the Tennessee side of the mountains, and a good number of cattle and hogs were driven over it in the fall.

Dr. John Jacob Mingus, a son of the first permanent settler, had a mill built on Mingus Creek

The Oconaluftee Pioneer Farmstead is a working farm where crops are grown and livestock raised (left). HOWARD KELLEY.

The old livestock varieties that mountain people favored are still raised at the farmstead (above). HOWARD KELLEY.

where corn and wheat could be ground into meal and flour. The turbine-powered mill, located a half-mile from Oconaluftee Visitor Center, was quite an advancement in its day. A visit to the working mill is an educational experience, and fresh, stoneground cornmeal can be purchased.

Three miles beyond Oconaluftee is Smokemont Campground, site of Champion Fibre Company's booming sawmill town in the 1920s. By 1925 more than 116 million board feet of lumber—hemlock, spruce, poplar, oak, ash, and cherry—had been removed from this area. A three-quarter-mile, self-guiding nature trail leaves from the campground, traversing a hillside of second-growth forest that displays the land's recovery from the wounds of logging. In summer, after a heavy rain, the trail is lined with phantasmagoric mushrooms in all sizes, shapes and colors. 🍂

MINGUS MILL

In his soft North Carolina accent Jim O'Neal spoke with concern: "If a deer takes a drink out of the creek, I'm closed down." It was a drought summer in the Southeast, and he was speaking like a true miller concerned about only one thing—keeping his millstones grinding.

O'Neal demonstrates how Mingus Mill operates and produces fresh-ground cornmeal for visitors to purchase. To fullfill his mission, he needs enough water from Mingus Creek to flow through the redwood millrace, down into the penstock and to the steel turbine that powers the millstones. He is one of several millers who have counted on the water in Mingus Creek for a long time.

In 1886 Sion T. Earley built Mingus Mill for Dr. John Mingus. He carved his initials, STE, in the upper story dormer of the mill, where the great bolting chest once separated flour into four grades. The mill operated for more than fifty years, then closed in 1940. After some rehabilitation, Mingus Mill was reopened in 1968 by the National Park Service.

The cornmeal pouring into the cloth bag is still warm from contact with the great millstones. The century-old granite rounds came from the mountains nearby, and Jim O'Neal had just sharpened the cutting edges a few months earlier.

He says that "a blind man could run a mill" because it's 70 percent sound and 30 percent feel. If the meal is lukewarm to the touch and the sound of the grinding stones is a certain pitch, the stones have been set correctly.

DESTINATIONS
36

DRIVING DISTANCE FROM
(in miles)

Gatlinburg	1
Cherokee	33
Townsend	22

FACILITIES
None

HIGHLIGHTS
Auto tour with self-guiding booklet, hiking and horseback trails, waterfalls, historic structures.

roaring fork

If you've seen all the T-shirt shops, eaten all the sweets allowable, and have a morning or afternoon left, then Roaring Fork is the place for you. With little fanfare, only a few blocks from the tangle of Gatlinburg's main street, this motor nature trail takes you into a private green world.

A stop at the Noah "Bud" Ogle farm will acquaint you with the Ogles, one of the first families to settle in the outlying areas of Gatlinburg (then White Oak Flats). Noah and Cindy's 400-acre farm was large for the time, 1879. They were probably the envy of all

the neighbors because they had running water—at least a pioneer version of it. Water flowed from a spring through an open wooden trough into a log sink in the kitchen.

In a short distance the Roaring Fork Motor Nature Trail begins. It is a six-mile, one-way, paved road—top speed fifteen miles an hour—with frequent turnouts and parking places. Please note that the road is closed in winter, and is not open at any time to buses, motorhomes, or vehicles towing trailers.

You first travel through a delightful cove

hardwood forest, known best among foresters and cabinetmakers for its incredible diversity of deciduous trees. Here in the Smokies the cove hardwoods reach their glory. In these deep-soiled valleys at the base of the mountains, and on steeper hillsides too, grow beech, basswood, buckeye, cherry, oak, maple, ash, yellow-poplar, silverbell, redbud, dogwood, magnolia, and many, many others. Because fossils of these kinds of trees have been found dating back to dinosaur times, this forest type is now considered of great antiquity.

Farther on are the beginnings of trails which lead to Rainbow and Grotto Falls, and eventually to Mount LeConte. Along the Grotto Falls Trail is the spring that gives birth to the Roaring Fork. As you enter the watershed, eastern hemlock predominates, the tree common throughout the Park from 3,500 to 5,000 feet. In the lower elevations hemlock is most often found along the streams and cool ravines, and one giant near Brushy Mountain measures nearly twenty feet in circumference. Hemlock was a much-sought tree by lumber companies, and in the Little River watershed alone half a billion board feet of it were removed before cutting stopped.

Part of the motor nature trail is on the old roadbed which took the course of least resistance—along the stream—whenever it could. About 1850 the former road was built, with pick and shovel, to serve the twenty-five families then living in Roaring Fork.

Some of the first settlers, Alfred and Martha Reagan and Ephraim Bales, are buried in the Roaring Fork Cemetery. The weathered, tan headstones in this small cemetery silently reveal a great deal about the sorrows of mountain life, how short it could be in a place so far from medical help. One stone is inscribed "Emma Reagan, Born Nov. 17, 1915, Died Nov. 7, 1916." Another reads "Quentin Kermit Ogle, March 11, 1922-May 22, 1923."

The author of the Roaring Fork brochure said it well: "To realize how difficult life was for them is to see how easy it is for us. You will have traveled

Noah "Bud" Ogle was one of the most innovative home builders to live in the Roaring Fork area (far left). KEN L. JENKINS.

The Roaring Fork Motor Nature Trail will take you through a lush cove hardwood forest (above). JOHN NETHERTON.

By building their own small tub mills, mountain people could avoid paying tolls at the larger commercial mills (left).
KEN L. JENKINS.

through Roaring Fork without dropping a bead of sweat or straining one muscle. To the pioneer traveler, that feat would have been inconceivable." 🍂

DRIVING DISTANCE FROM
(in miles)
Gatlinburg   2
Cherokee   30
Townsend   18

FACILITIES
Visitor Center
Restrooms
Information and book sales outlet
Backcountry permits
Park headquarters

HIGHLIGHTS
Orientation program, publications, natural history exhibits, self-guiding nature trail, beginning of Newfound Gap Road across Park.

sugarlands

In the early part of this century, to reach Sugarlands, Tennessee, people first had to travel a dirt road to the small village of Gatlinburg and then ride a mule up the Old Sugarlands Road. This remote valley, which contained a few pioneer cabins and cornfields, was known on the North Carolina side of the mountains as Blockader's Glory or Moonshiner's Paradise.

Today, it's a different story. Of the ten million or so visits to Great Smoky Mountains National Park each year, about three-fourths begin at Sugarlands. Here you can find a large Park Service Visitor Center, open year-round, with programs, exhibits, publications, and rangers who will answer your questions. The latest issue of the free Park newspaper is also available, containing timely information on facilities, ranger-led walks and talks, and articles on topics of interest in the Park. If you're looking for a campsite, you can find the daily status of each of the Park's ten campgrounds posted at Sugarlands Visitor Center.

Sugarlands is a good place to get started, to sort out the myriad ways you might begin to explore the Park's half-million acres. It's also a good place to

*Sugarlands Visitor Center features
extraordinary exhibits of plants and animals
from throughout the Park (left).*
NATIONAL PARK SERVICE.

*The sugar maple trees from which residents
gathered sap lent this valley its name
(right).* JOHN NETHERTON.

stretch your legs and take an easy walk on the Sugarlands Nature Trail, just behind the Visitor Center.

The community of Forks of the River occupied the land where the Visitor Center now sits. A Baptist church was located near the present Park Headquarters building, and the Bridge Schoolhouse stood close by. Caleb Trentham set up one of the first sawmills about 1868, and a grist mill was also operating. The site of Noah McCarter's two-story weatherboard house is marked now only by a pile of stones and some telltale plants—a walnut tree, some yuccas, and a large boxwood bush. But John Ownby's restored cabin, of yellow-poplar and white pine, hints at the more extensive collection of log buildings and other historic structures to be seen at Cades Cove, Cataloochee, and Roaring Fork.

Should you desire a longer hike, check at the backcountry station near the beginning of the Nature Trail. Overnight hikes in Great Smokies require a permit, available through a self-registration system. The backcountry station at Sugarlands has permit forms and possible itineraries for all areas of the Park.

If you wish to drive through the Park, the Newfound Gap Road (U.S. 441) begins at Sugarlands. Only a few miles up this road is the Carlos Campbell Overlook, offering a rare and spectacular view of five distinct forest types. The twenty-six-mile Newfound Gap Road leads to the Oconaluftee Visitor Center, Blue Ridge Parkway, and Cherokee, North Carolina. The publication *Mountain Roads & Quiet Places,* available at the book sales area in Sugarlands and other Park visitor centers, is a complete guide to the roads in the Park and is an excellent companion for a driving tour of the Smokies. 🍁

DESTINATIONS
40

FACILITIES
Campgrounds
Picnic area
Restrooms

HIGHLIGHTS
Views of Smoky Mountains from perimeter.

foothills parkway, west & east

The Foothills Parkway is noted for its exceptional views and splendid autumn colors. FRANCES DORRIS.

The Foothills Parkway offers a good alternative to the heavily traveled Park roads, and both the east and west sections provide fine views of the mountains. Overlooks along the thirteen-mile parkway on the west side, particularly, afford some stupendous vistas of the Smokies skyline, and this stretch is a "hot spot" for fall colors. Look Rock Campground, open in summer, is located midway along the west side, and Abrams Creek Campground is at its southern end near Chilhowee Reservoir.

The six-mile Foothills Parkway East connects to Interstate 40 and gives access to Big Creek and Cataloochee in Great Smoky Mountains National Park. It also affords some fine views, but is closed in winter. ❧

big creek

Big Creek is a quiet hideaway especially favored by hikers and horseback riders.
JOHN MINCEY.

Big Creek is a tiny campground—only nine sites— in the northeast corner of the Smokies between Cosby and Cataloochee. Traces of the previous Civilian Conservation Corps and logging camps are obvious in the area. The Chestnut Ridge Trail at Big Creek provides a short connection to the Appalachian Trail and to Mount Cammerer, one of the best high views in the Park. Another popular hike from Big Creek Campground is to Walnut Bottoms.

twentymile

You can count on having the beauty of this corner of the Smokies pretty much to yourself if you make the pilgrimage to the remote Twentymile area. FRANCES DORRIS.

Twentymile is located near Fontana Dam in the far southwest corner of the Park. Here you may park your vehicle and head out on hiking trails into this roadless part of the Great Smokies—to Shuckstack on the Appalachian Trail via the Twentymile Trail. Wolf Ridge Trail, which also departs here, passes by Parson Bald and connects with several other trails. Gregory Bald, with renowned flame azalea displays in early summer, can be reached via Twentymile, Long Hungry Ridge, and Wolf Ridge trails.

DRIVING DISTANCE FROM
(in miles)
Gatlinburg 29
Cherokee 62
Townsend 50

FACILITIES
Campground
Restrooms
Ranger station
Hiking trails
Picnic area
Horsecamp

HIGHLIGHTS
Fishing, hiking, swimming.

DRIVING DISTANCE FROM
(in miles)
Gatlinburg 61
Cherokee 56
Townsend 41 (31 via Parson Branch Road)

FACILITIES
Ranger station
Restrooms
Backcountry permits

HIGHLIGHTS
Hiking trails, near manmade lakes.

opportunities

Sugarlands Visitor Center, near Gatlinburg, Tennessee (above, left). HOWARD KELLEY.

Oconaluftee Visitor Center, near Cherokee, North Carolina (above, right). HOWARD KELLEY.

Cades Cove Visitor Center, on the west end of the Park (right). NATIONAL PARK SERVICE.

visitor centers

Where to begin? Great Smoky Mountains National Park can be bewildering for the first-time visitor. To make the most of your time here, start at one of the three Park visitor centers. At all the centers you may obtain Park maps and the Park newspaper, which carries the schedule of daily activities. Bulletin boards also post additional information on activities, campgrounds, and other pertinent matters. All the visitor centers have restrooms and drinking water.

SUGARLANDS: Near Gatlinburg, the Sugarlands Visitor Center features exhibits, orientation film, book sales area, and friendly rangers to answer your questions. Exhibits in the newly redesigned center feature illustrations by John Dawson, photographs by Eliot Porter, and full-size mounted specimens of the plants and animals you might see in the Park's several ecosystems. This museum invites you to browse and wander, as if you were going from Sugarlands up to Mount LeConte or Clingmans Dome. Sugarlands is open all year, except Christmas Day.

OCONALUFTEE: In this lovely old stone and chestnut building visitors are welcomed to the North Carolina side of the Park. Exhibits reinforce the area's theme of pioneer life. Nearby is the Pioneer Farmstead, with living history demonstrations, and a half-mile away is the water-powered Mingus Mill. A ranger station and restrooms are available at Oconaluftee, and a book sales area offers many selections on natural history and crafts. Oconaluftee is open year-round, except Christmas Day.

CADES COVE: Located in the Cable Mill area on the Cades Cove Loop Road, this visitor center offers a look at life in this once-thriving pioneer community. Information, exhibits, and a sales area can be found here. Tours of the working grist mill begin outside the visitor center. The visitor center is open from mid-April through October. 🍁

camping

Camping boils down life to the essentials—staying dry, staying warm, and staying fed. Why modern man and woman choose to engage in this ancient practice is perhaps a mystery to many. But we still do, undoubtedly in large part because of camping's simplicity and small but infinite pleasures.

Where else can you have a woodpecker for an alarm clock? And where can you spend your nights contemplating the stars, smelling the sweet aroma of wood smoke, and listening to a stream gurgle just outside your door? Or have a skunk as a campmate?

All these and more are the fringe benefits of camping out in the Smoky Mountains.

There are developed campgrounds in various corners of Great Smoky Mountains National Park. Three—Elkmont, Smokemont, and Cades Cove—are the largest and most fully developed. They are open year-round. At the time of this writing, advance reservations are available—and necessary—from May through October at these three campgrounds and can be made through a reservation system. Because the system is subject to change it is advisable to check

Camping allows you to linger long enough to enjoy the Smokies more subtle wonders, like this maidenhair fern (left). JOHN NETHERTON.

Camping means trying those culinary delights you might ordinarily miss at home (right). HOWARD KELLEY.

The Smokies' famous rainfalls bring out the innovativeness in campers (left).

HOWARD KELLEY.

First published in 1907, Horace Kephart's book tells how to do everything from making a fire to building and furnishing a cabin (right).

each year for current information. Contact Superintendent, Great Smoky Mountains National Park, Gatlinburg, TN 37738, Telephone (615) 436-1200.

Four campgrounds—Cosby, Balsam Mountain, Deep Creek, and Look Rock—have sites available on a first-come, first-serve basis. The three smallest campgrounds—Abrams Creek, Big Creek, and Cataloochee—are also first-come, first-serve. Differences among the campgrounds have more to do with size, remoteness, and space for recreational vehicles than with amenities. All the campgrounds are equipped with restrooms, flush toilets, running water, picnic tables, and cooking grates. None have hookups,

showers, or laundries, though these facilities are available at nearby towns and in commercial campgrounds outside the Park. The camp store at Cades Cove offers a limited stock of food and supplies. It is the only such store in the Park, and is closed in winter.

Backcountry camping is also possible in the Great Smokies, and is discussed in more detail in the Hiking section on page 54.

If you're a first-time camper, you face some decisions regarding proper and necessary equipment. What do you really need and how much should you spend? There is a wealth of equipment around these days, some more worthwhile than others. Before you empty your checking account, seek advice from a seasoned camper or a responsible sales person at a good sporting goods store.

Keep in mind the basics. In the Smokies you'll need a good tent that will keep you dry for several days, even after those inevitable, all-night rains. That good old surplus canvas tent may not be the best choice here. The miracle fabric—nylon—has much to recommend it, with a good rain fly for a cover. And don't forget to check the zipper on the doors.

For sleeping bags, you may still have in the attic those nice cloth bags with ducks on the flannel lining. Again, however, big improvements have been made in lightweight, water-resistant, synthetic materials. Determine how warm and dry you really want to be and choose the best bag within your budget.

As a camper friend has observed, over the past twenty years the ground has definitely gotten harder. I concur wholeheartedly. If you're young, you can probably get away with sleeping on the bare tent floor or with a flimsy little pad. If you're over thirty, consider investing in one of those thermal inflatable pads. They're worth every penny.

For cooking, you may wish to use only campfires. They are allowed in the campgrounds and backcountry in the Smokies, with *dead and down* wood only. But soggy wood, of which there is an abundance, is tough to ignite. Dry firewood, already split, can be purchased at a few campgrounds, but if you're camping for any length of time this may become a substantial expense.

The solution is to bring a portable propane or gasoline stove, now available in several makes and models. If you're resurrecting an old one, be sure to test it before you leave home to make sure it's in good working order. Cold suppers can get mighty lonely after a while.

Veteran Smokies campers, I've noticed, include an item that seems most worthwhile—a tarp to cover the picnic table area so they can eat out of the rain. If you want to get really fancy you can bring lawn chairs, lanterns, tablecloths, portable sinks, hammocks, saws—the list of amenities is endless, of course, and subject to personal whim. Each camper has his or her favorite toys, but additional material goods seem only to detract from the inherent beauty of the activity—simplicity.

A few words about camp etiquette are in order. Most people come here to get away from it all, for a little peace and quiet. Generally they are an early-to-bed, early-to-rise bunch, so please respect fellow campers. Quiet hours are in effect at all campgrounds from 10 p.m. until 6 a.m. Barking dogs, unrestrained children, and loud generators are not conducive to a pleasant camping experience. (Pets must be on a leash or in a cage at all times.) Please don't shine car lights, flashlights, or lanterns in other people's campsites.

Try to leave the campsite cleaner than when you arrived. Dispose of all trash in the bearproof garbage cans, and dump all dishwater and minor food residue in the utility sinks at the restrooms. When you leave, douse your campfire and double-check the site to make sure you haven't overlooked something that you'll remember when you're 200 miles down the road.

And it can't be said often enough, it seems—DON'T feed bears or other wildlife. I watched with

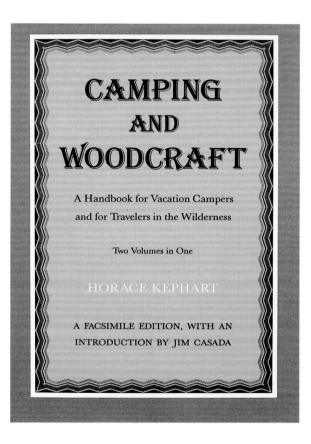

disbelief as a young girl next to my camp in Cades Cove offered her banana to a skunk one morning. The same skunk, I am certain, had been snuffling around my tent the previous night. I'm happy to report that the curious marauder continued on to happier hunting grounds.

Had it been a black bear visiting my next-door-neighbor's camp instead, I shudder to think of the consequences. Unfortunately, bears have learned to associate food with humans, especially at campgrounds and picnic areas. To avoid problems for you and the bear, stow all your food and cooking gear out of sight in the trunk of your vehicle. 🍁

BRUNSWICK STEW

Horace Kephart, a Park advocate who lived in the Smokies in the early 1900s, wrote a little classic called *The Book of Camping and Woodcraft*. It offered lots of advice for happy campers. For clothing he recommended pure, soft wool underwear and leggings, a silk neckerchief, and an old business suit. "The best coffee or tea this side of Elysium," wrote Kephart, "is brewed . . . in a tightly lidded pail." And the staple food for all campers was pork and beans, to "sustain a man from six to ten hours."

Kephart also included a recipe for Brunswick Stew. We pass it on here for the possible enjoyment of modern-day campers. Feel free to substitute other meat for the "several squirrels" called for in this recipe:

1 qt. can tomatoes,
1 pt. can butter beans or limas,
1 pt. can green corn,
6 potatoes, parboiled and sliced,
1/2 lb. butter,
1/2 lb. salt pork (fat),
1 teaspoonful black pepper,
1/2 teaspoonful Cayenne,
1 tablespoonful salt,
2 tablespoonfuls white sugar,
1 onion, minced small

Soak the squirrels half an hour in cold salted water. Add the salt to one gallon of water, and boil five minutes. Then put in the onion, beans, corn, pork (cut in fine strips), potatoes, pepper, and squirrels. Cover closely, and stew very slowly two-and-a-half hours, stirring frequently. Add the tomatoes and sugar, and stew an hour longer. Then add the butter, cut into bits the size of a walnut and roll in flour. Boil ten minutes.

photography

A macro lens works well for photographing the Smokies' intriguing salamanders (left).
JOHN NETHERTON.

Autumn leaves don't have to be photographed only on the trees (right).
JOHN NETHERTON.

Nature photographer Thomas W. Martin says that when he looks through the lens of his camera he can imagine how a violinist feels as he takes up a bow: "The beauties of nature that I see are surely akin to great music."

The Smoky Mountains offer a symphony of subjects for nature photographers of all levels of expertise. From panoramic mountains to the tiniest insect, the variety and detail are infinite. Armed with a camera and a few tips from the experts, almost anyone can begin to practice this different way of hunting, embarking on a new way of seeing nature and the out-of-doors.

In the nineteenth century, when photography was born, practitioners of the craft lugged huge cameras and glass plates all over the countryside. Since that time modern technology has presented us with smaller cameras, interchangeable lenses, and all manner of filters and fast films. Now, with compact, light cameras we can penetrate some of the wildest parts of the country—photographing birds in flight, insects at close range, and fish swimming underwater.

The Smoky Mountains have prompted a new generation of photographers to reach stunning heights in the medium. One is Nashvillian John Netherton, who with David Duhl has written an entire book on the subject, entitled *A Guide to Photography and the Smoky Mountains*. The book contains advice for both novices and professionals. Here are some of Netherton's tips that will help you begin to achieve more satisfying results with your photography.

The low-light conditions that prevail in the forests of the Smokies, and the long shutter speeds that are often required, make use of a tripod mandatory. A polarizing filter on a lens helps eliminate unwanted reflections from streams, wet rocks, and leaves, and will also give bluer skies.

Adjustments of the aperture setting can enrich colors, especially if you are using slide film. Underexpose a third or a half stop, unless you are shooting snow or fog; in these cases, overexposing a half stop or more will compensate for the meter reading of such bright backgrounds.

To show motion and obtain that silken effect of waterfalls, use shutter speeds of a half second or more. To stop the water's motion, use a shutter speed of 1/60 of a second or faster. Be aware when taking pictures of waterfalls, or when shooting in the rain, that drops of water on the lens will show up as blurred spots on the final picture.

Nature photographers can't be fair-weather people. If you avoid rainy days, or cold weather, or other times when most people are sitting inside by the fire, you'll miss some striking photo opportunities. Just carry along a plastic trash bag to cover the camera or mount an umbrella on the tripod. On overcast days, colors are richer and more saturated.

To capture long mountain panoramas change to a telephoto lens, which compresses the scene and gives force to the mountains. In contrast, closeups of wildflowers require a different approach. To counteract wind or even the slightest vibration from your

own body, mount the camera on a tripod. Use a 200mm macro lens or an 80 to 200mm zoom with a bellows. At times a whole hillside or field of flowers is desirable, in which case you will want to switch to a wide-angle lens.

Wildlife photography is a specialty within nature photography that asks much patience and knowledge of animal habits. In photographing any animals, sharply focus on the eyes. Should you have an opportunity to photograph a bear, do so from a distance using a medium telephoto lens. No matter how good the picture, don't ever come between a sow and her cubs. Deer are skittish and often require long waiting periods and a long lens. If you want

By using a tripod you can shoot streams at slow shutter speeds and capture the blur of motion. FRANCES DORRIS.

OPPORTUNITIES

50

Selecting the right background is an important consideration when photographing wildflowers. JOHN NETHERTON.

to photograph birds in flight, you'll probably need a motor drive with shutter speed preset at 1/500 or 1/1000 of a second. Salamanders, in which the Smokies are especially rich, are nocturnal creatures. To photograph them, Netherton recommends a two-unit flash system, set at low angles. Using a flash while shooting nightime animals will also blacken the background, ridding the photograph of distracting elements.

In October, roadsides in the Smokies are full of odd, five-legged creatures—photographers with tripods—focusing on the once-a-year spectacle of autumn foliage. For the best fall photos, shoot after a rain, isolating areas of color rather than trying to get whole hillsides. Colorful leaves set against dark evergreens are especially effective. And omit the blue sky from the picture, which will only detract from the drama.

Sunrises and sunsets are perennially popular subjects as well. A good place to photograph sunrise is from Newfound Gap or Clingmans Dome. But be there early, thirty to forty-five minutes before actual sunrise. Sunsets from Mount LeConte are also recommended. ✤

The Smokies can boast hundreds of miles of cool, clear trout streams. HOWARD KELLEY.

OPPORTUNITIES
51

fishing

God meant for some people to fish. Though I may not have been one of them, at least I was determined to try. And the fast-water streams in the Smoky Mountains were touted as the crème de la crème of flyfishing in the eastern United States. So, why not start at the top?

To get started, though, I had a lot to learn. First, I had to decipher the jargon of the sport and decide on some minimal equipment—which pole, which reel, which line, which flies. Now this can be daunting to the beginner. You have your graphite rods, both long and short, your dry flies and wet flies, and your No. 4 or your No. 5 line. Selecting the flies was like being let loose in a candy store. I chose a dozen or so—Adams and Wulffs and Royal Coachman and others. (In the national park, fishing with bait is prohibited. Only artificial flies or lures with a single hook may be used.) Once all the basic gear was assembled, I had to withstand the temptation of a pair of waders, a lovely woven creel, and one of those nice vests with all the pockets.

I also had to pretend I didn't hear the doubtful

OPPORTUNITIES
52

The cane pole, standard angling gear for early mountain people, still works wonders today. HOWARD KELLEY.

tone in friends' voices when they asked if I'd ever flyfished before. "Do you know how to cast?" they inquired circumspectly. "No," I replied confidently, "but I'm sure I can learn." There can't be that much to it, I thought, though I didn't say that aloud. "Practice in the backyard," they said.

I began to gain an inkling of the purism (dare I say elitism?) that surrounds this sport. Of course, they may have sensed my selfish motivation—I love to eat fresh trout. I learned quickly that you just don't risk the scorn of these people by admitting openly to this weakness in character. Many flyfishermen would sooner reveal their favorite fishing hole than keep—or eat—the fish they catch.

Finally the big day arrived. Of the more than 700 miles of fishable water in 300 odd creeks in Great Smoky Mountains National Park, I chose Deep Creek as the place of initiation. A magazine article said that many southern flyfishermen consider it and Hazel Creek as the two best trout streams in the Smokies.

So, how could I lose? I bought a license at the hardware store in Bryson City and met a friend early one Saturday morning at the campground. We walked up the creek, studying the pools to see where the fish were and checking under rocks to find what insects were hatching.

Rainbow trout, which like the fast water in plunge pools below falls, are the dominant species in many Smokies streams. Brown trout, introduced into the Tennessee Valley in 1900, have spread into the mountains. They're found in larger streams at lower elevations in the Park and often lurk at the outer edges of pools, around rocks and tree roots.

The other trout is the brook, or "spec," as it's known. The native brookies have retreated to the headwaters of the streams in the Smokies, losing ground due to the effects of early logging and competition from the rainbows and browns. In 1975 the National Park Service declared brook trout off limits to fishermen. A brook trout restoration project

has begun which involves placing the introduced species downstream, below waterfalls that are barriers to their upstream movements. If successful, this program may allow anglers to fish for the much-coveted "spec" once again.

After we had gone far enough, we clambered through the brush to the streamside, tied a Tellico nymph on our hooks, and tried to keep a low profile. The wily trout are sensitive to shadows, my friend advised. This was my first real try at casting in the wild, and I quickly realized the value of diligent practice. My line straggled a few feet out in the water, and any trout worth its fins would have known what was up.

I tried to imitate the grace of my companion's arm movements as he skillfully cast the fly exactly where he wanted it on the water. We fished this spot for an hour or so, without a nibble. What my friend said he liked about trout fishing, and what I hadn't realized before, was what it can teach a person about the natural world—how fish think.

Perhaps I will pursue the challenge—learning how a fish thinks—and perhaps learn more about myself in the process.

Fishing Tips

In his *Smoky Mountains Trout Fishing Guide,* Don Kirk offers these tactics and tips for trout fishing in the Smokies. Observe where the trout position themselves in a stream as they wait for food. Smokies trout are opportunistic feeders, and will eat anything that is hatching—mayflies, caddis flies, stone flies, midges, and some terrestrial insects—in a few hours' time. This knowledge and an examination of stomach contents will help you know what fly to use. Spring and fall are busy times in the trout world, and in winter the trout, though more torpid, will seek sunlit areas on milder days.

If you fish facing upstream, the same direction the trout are facing, you conceal your presence by

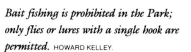

Bait fishing is prohibited in the Park; only flies or lures with a single hook are permitted. HOWARD KELLEY.

coming up quietly from behind. On small streams, sidearm casts will probably be necessary to avoid overhanging trees. When you cast, try to place the fly along the edges of waterfalls, letting the current carry it to the end of a pool.

While many will choose the best fly rod money can buy, a cane pole is legendarily as good a rod as any for fishing in these mountains. For lures, spinners rather than flies have been used to catch some notably big fish in the Park.

Favorite areas for rainbow trout include the Little River, Abrams, Hazel, and Bradley creeks, the Oconaluftee River, and Big Creek.

A valid Tennessee or North Carolina fishing license, which can be purchased at local sporting goods stores, will allow you to fish anywhere in the Park. Current fishing regulations and stream closures can be obtained by writing to Great Smoky Mountains National Park, Gatlinburg, Tennessee 37738; also, check bulletin boards in the Park. ❧

Hiking lets you explore the Smokies with all your senses (left). FRANCES DORRIS.

A short walk can show you a side of the Park you could never experience from your car (right). FRANCES DORRIS.

hiking

The view from Brushy Mountain that October day was mesmerizing. Clouds roared through Trillium Gap and wisps of fog clung to the trees like angel hair. Brushy is crowned by a heath bald, a Lilliputian world of stunted sand myrtle, blueberry, rhododendron, and laurel. The rhododendron and laurel were deep green and the leaves of the blueberry bushes had turned red. Amid the gray fog I felt I had arrived in Norway at Christmastime.

An enthusiastic group of local hikers exclaimed as the clouds selectively revealed familiar peaks on the mainline crest of the Smokies. A raven pirouetted over Porters Flat. Suddenly the sweeping flanks of Mount LeConte were exposed, covered with hoarfrost. The temperature up here at 4,910 feet was 27 degrees. On LeConte, almost 1,500 feet higher, it was chilly enough to condense and freeze the moisture in the clouds.

The unexpected rewards of this nine-mile hike to Brushy Mountain are possible only with some effort. But they are worth every step. This jaunt is one of a lifetime's worth of hikes waiting for you on the

900 miles of trail in Great Smoky Mountains National Park. People of any age can hike to peaks, balds, and waterfalls, to see wildflowers, virgin trees, salamanders, and sunsets. You may go for an hour, a half day, overnight, for a week, or for a month.

But you don't have to start with nine miles in a day. An excellent place to begin is on the Quiet Walkways that depart from major roads in the Park. These are easy trails often a half mile or so and there's no need to strap on hiking boots or a backpack. In only a short distance these walkways take you light years away from the crowds and traffic. Find one that looks interesting, take lunch, sit on a log, and listen to the stream trickle. You'll probably have the place all to yourself.

Other recommended short hikes are possible along the self-guiding nature trails in the Park. With brochure in hand, you may linger at the numbered stops along the way and acquaint yourself with the diverse biology and human history of the Smoky Mountains. You will find these well-marked, easy-to-follow trails at Smokemont, Elkmont, Sugarlands, Cades Cove, Laurel Falls, and several other places.

DAYHIKES: Given the multitude of choices for hikes, we offer a few suggestions for longer dayhikes in various sections of the Park:

Smokemont Loop, Smokemont Campground: A fairly easy six-mile roundtrip hike through cove hardwood and hemlock forests. Historic homesites and a cemetery can also be seen. Starts near Campsite D-19.

Mount Cammerer, Cosby Campground: A longer hike, about 12 miles roundtrip, to a fire tower atop Mount Cammerer, one of the best views in the Park.

Boogerman Trail, Cataloochee Campground: From Caldwell Fork this loop trail traverses a forest of big trees in a remote part of the Park; 7½ miles roundtrip.

Rainbow Falls, Cherokee Orchard Road (near Gatlinburg): A moderate 5½-mile roundtrip hike to a lovely, 80-foot-high waterfall. If you're still going

strong at the falls, you can continue for another 4 miles to the top of Mount LeConte.

Rich Mountain Loop, Cades Cove: This moderate, 7½-mile roundtrip loop trail starts across the road from the orientation shelter at the start of the Cades Cove Loop Road. An especially good hike for wildflowers in spring and early summer and leaf colors in autumn.

Silers Bald, Clingmans Dome: This hike affords both a visit to a grassy bald and a hike on a portion of the Appalachian Trail. Eight miles roundtrip, west on the Appalachian Trail from Clingmans Dome.

Shuckstack, Twentymile: In a wild part of the Park's southwest corner, this 10-mile roundtrip hike ends at a fire tower atop Shuckstack, on the Appalachian Trail. Offers "one of the most extraordinary panoramic views of the Southern Appalachians," says the trail guide.

When planning a hike, have in mind what you hope to see: waterfalls, views, streams, virgin forests, or balds. HOWARD KELLEY.

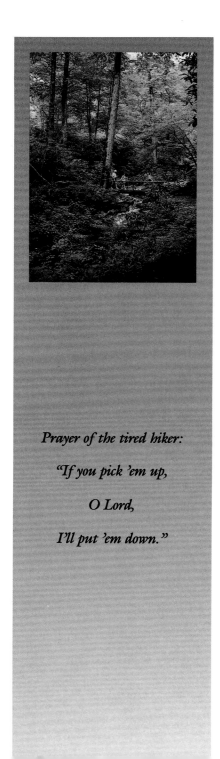

Prayer of the tired hiker:

"If you pick 'em up,

O Lord,

I'll put 'em down."

OVERNIGHT HIKES: Extended backcountry hiking is available almost without end in the Smokies. First, get the Park's official trail map, which contains the most current information on mileages, campsites, trip planning, and permits. With it and the proper topographic maps, you'll be well-armed to hike in the backcountry. The Sierra Club's *Hiker's Guide to the Smokies* is a good basic book, but some changes have occurred since it was last updated.

All overnight hiking and camping requires a free permit, which you obtain by self-registering at any ranger station. Trip planning is essential because you must camp in designated backcountry campsites, and use at some campsites is rationed (as indicated on trail map). If your trip includes a stay at a rationed site, you must telephone the backcountry office to register. Telephone Park Headquarters at (615) 436-1200 to get the current number. Reservations a month in advance are recommended for rationed sites. The backcountry office is happy to advise hikers on itineraries, lesser-used trails, and any other matters.

Backcountry campsites are spaced so that you can stay within the recommended eight to ten miles a day maximum length. Some eighteen shelters are also maintained in the Park. These are three-sided lean-tos with bunks, and some have wire on the fourth side to prevent bear entry.

Safety is a primary concern in the backcountry. Rule number one is DON'T HIKE ALONE. If you must, let someone know your plans. This is rugged, forested country and you can become lost easily. The best precaution is to STAY ON THE TRAILS. Should you become lost, stay where you are. Your chances of being found by searchers are greatly increased.

The two main causes of deaths among Smokies hikers are falls (primarily from climbing on rocks around waterfalls) and hypothermia. The precaution against the first accident is obvious. Hypothermia, or "exposure," is a more subtle danger, and the Smokies offer ideal conditions for its occurrence. The body's core temprature is lowered when you are exposed to wind, rain, and cold. It's late in the day, you're wet from rain or from sweat, the wind comes up, and it's 30 to 50 degrees Fahrenheit outside. Beware. These are ideal hypothermia conditions. By the time symptoms appear—shivering, stumbling, slurred speech, drowsiness—you are already in danger. Put on dry clothes, hat, gloves, windbreaker, drink warm fluids, and seek shelter. If someone in your group is exhibiting symptoms, get the person to shelter and into a sleeping bag immediately. Body-to-body contact could also save someone.

Sanitation is a major problem in a place as heavily used as the Smokies backcountry. Proper disposal of human wastes is extremely important. You must bury your feces in a six-inch hole, at least 100 feet away from trail, camp, and water source. Pack out all your trash.

Bring all water from any source to a boil for at least a full minute. Though the streams look pure, they may contain viruses and bacteria that can turn a pleasant trip into a disaster.

APPALACHIAN TRAIL: In founder Benton MacKaye's words, the ultimate purpose of the Appalachian Trail is "To walk. To see. And to *see* what you see." Founded in 1921 and maintained by volunteers, the Appalachian Trail is a 2,000-mile footpath from Maine to Georgia. The "AT" holds an irresistible attraction to hikers. It offers challenge and adventure, and a comradery develops along this green corridor that is one of its treasured values. But in the Smokies, it's crowded. Hundreds of people trod the AT in the Park, so be forewarned that most sections won't offer a true wilderness experience by a long shot.

Seventy of the Appalachian Trail's 2,000 miles cross the Smoky Mountains from Davenport Gap on the east to Fontana Dam at the southwest edge of the Park. Newfound Gap Road provides paved access at about the halfway point. Distinctive white blazes mark the AT's route across the crest of the Great Smokies on the Tennessee-North Carolina border. It passes near or goes up to several of the highest peaks in the eastern United States, including Mounts Cammerer, Guyot, and Chapman, Charlie's Bunion, Clingmans Dome, Thunderhead Mountain, and Shuckstack. The AT meanders through those grassy meadows called balds and drops down into gaps where other trails join and head to the low country.

The best source on mileages, water sources, shelters, and other details is *A Guide to the Appalachian Trail in the Southern Appalachians*, published and periodically updated by the Appalachian Trail Conference located in Harpers Ferry, West Virginia. It can be purchased at Park visitor centers. ❧

In the Smokies, over 800 miles of hiking trails offer a lifetime's worth of enjoyment and adventure (sidebar). HOWARD KELLEY.

Hydro-therapy for trail-weary feet is rarely far away (far left). HOWARD KELLEY.

Seventy of the Appalachian Trail's 2,000 miles run through the Smokies (above). HOWARD KELLEY.

Waterfalls, which provide natural air conditioning on hot summer days, are a favorite destination for hikers (left). JOHN NETHERTON.

OPPORTUNITIES
58

horseback riding

The Park's five commercial stables provide opportunities for horseback riding along a variety of scenic trails (left). HOWARD KELLEY.

Horseback riding preserves a traditional mode of transportation in these mountains (right). FRANCES DORRIS.

The brochure said "you will find our horses gentle, the trails easy and the scenery simply beautiful." It was that part about gentle horses that attracted me most. I knew the other two would be true.

So on a fine fall Sunday I swung myself up in the saddle, whispered sweet nothings to my trusty steed, and asked his name. "Chasteen," replied the wrangler, which sounded pretty dignified (and gentle) to me. "But his nickname is 'Noodles,' " he added. Oh well, I thought, so much for dignity.

But Chasteen seemed fine, maybe a little less sure footed than I would have liked as we set out over the rocky portion of the trail near Smokemont Campground. It was late afternoon, and Chasteen had probably already put in a good day's work. He stayed within a horsehair of the mount in front, so I had to pull back continually on the reins.

These were minor matters though. It was a quintessential autumn day in the Smoky Mountains— they don't come much better. We moseyed up Bradley Fork, smelling the leaves, studying the forest, listening to the creek, and asking our guide a few questions.

A horseback ride will take you deep into the heart of the Smokies. JOHN NETHERTON.

We headed left on an unmarked side trail and in four miles ended at our destination, Chasteen Falls. We tied the horses to the hitching post, and as I dismounted I seemed to be having problems straightening out my legs. Our guide motioned in the direction of the falls. "Stretch your legs," he said. Good idea, I thought.

Seeing the Smokies by horseback is an adventure, especially for those of us who spend most of our lives using other modes of transportation. Possibilities to do so are available through five commercial riding stables scattered through the Park, including the one at Smokemont, two near Gatlinburg, and others at Cosby and Cades Cove.

These are private concessions operating within the National Park, thus they set their own rules about who can ride and when. Standard day trips with a guide are priced by the hour, and longer trips are available by special arrangement through the individual stables. The age limit generally is five years old. If you are interested in horseback riding in the Park, check with the stables when you arrive. Addresses may be obtained in advance from the Superintendent, Great Smoky Mountains National Park, Gatlinburg, TN 37738, (615) 436-1200, or through local chambers of commerce.

You may also ride your own horse in the Park on designated horse trails, which are shown on the Park trail map. Frontcountry (with drive-in access) and backcountry horsecamps are available, but need to be reserved in advance through the Backcountry Reservations Office. Call (615) 436-1200 for the current number. All stock feed must be packed in and packed out if unused. 🍁

Bicycling in the Smokies can be exhilarating, but opportunities are mostly limited to Cades Cove and Cataloochee (left). HOWARD KELLEY.

Bicycling Cades Cove at dawn is a pleasure you will never forget (right). KEN L. JENKINS.

bicycling

You know what they say: It's like riding a bicycle. You never forget. And they're right. So dust off the old bone-shaker, grease the chain, and pump up the tires. See the Smokies in a different way—from the seat of a bicycle.

More specifically, see Cades Cove early on a Saturday morning in summer when the eleven-mile loop road is closed to vehicles. If you camp at Cades Cove the night before, you'll have a jump on the crowds who elect to see this beautiful valley under their own power. Vehicles are prohibited on the road

from 7 a.m. until 10 a.m., so you'll want to get up with the robins for your bike, jog, or walk. One-speed bicycles can be rented at the camp store.

One August morning I rented a bike and pedaled off into the sunrise. The cove was filled with fog, tinted a soft apricot by the dawn rays, and only the tops of Thunderhead and the other presiding mountains were visible. The mist was so thick that I was soon bathed in it. Cotton nets of spider webs knit the grasses together. Diamonds of dew dripped off the tips of the hemlock needles, and lichen

spattered the tree trunks. Four white-tailed deer nibbled grasses in a meadow, oblivious to my passing.

This was paradise. No fumes, no traffic jams, friendly folks greeting each other good morning— what some of us dream of in a utopian future. The chain on my bicycle clattered noisily, and I wanted to apologize for disturbing the utterly silent morning.

There are plenty of places to stop along the way, even if you don't need a break—the Primitive Baptist Church, Cable Mill, the Dan Lawson place. But pull off the road so that you don't block the way for people riding up behind you. Use caution as you approach steep, downhill grades. If you're accustomed to riding a ten-speed, remember that the rental bikes have those old-fashioned foot brakes, not hand brakes. Please observe signs that say "Walk Your Bike." There are a few ascents too; just take your time and stop to inhale the fresh air and enjoy the scenery. The graveled Sparks and Hyatt lanes allow shortcuts across the cove, should you not wish to ride the full distance.

This Saturday morning special is really the only recommended bicycle ride in the Park. Other roads are narrow and winding, with skinny shoulders. Bicycling on them can be hazardous to your health. Some people do ride bicycles around the campgrounds, which looks safe enough. A few lesser-traveled, gravel backroads, like Parson Branch and Rich Mountain, are suitable for mountain bikes. 🍁

The off-season is another good time to pedal the cove (left). FRANCES DORRIS.

Bicycling improves your chances of seeing deer, raccoons, turkeys, and other wildlife (right). FRANCES DORRIS.

learning

Park Rangers conduct special walks, talks, and evening campfire programs from spring through autumn (left). NATIONAL PARK SERVICE.

A variety of educational programs allows visitors to learn some of the secrets of the Great Smoky Mountains (right). JOHN NETHERTON.

A poster on the wall at the Great Smoky Mountains Institute at Tremont reads: "The most important education of all comes from reading the language of rocks and mountains, enjoying the music of streams and forests, understanding the message of cricket and owl."

This seemed to me a fine expression of the philosophy of education in the national parks. That philosophy is put into practice in Great Smoky Mountains National Park in many ways.

First and most visible to visitors are the ranger-led programs. Free guided walks and talks are held daily in various locations throughout the Park. There are talks on bears, walks along streams, twilight strolls, storytellings, and hayrides, to name only a few. A full listing of programs, times, and meeting places is carried in the "Smokies Guide," the free Park newspaper, and is posted on bulletin boards. In addition, there is always that great Park Service tradition—evening campfire programs at the amphitheaters at Smokemont, Elkmont, Cosby, Deep Creek, Balsam Mountain, and Cades Cove campgrounds.

Self-guiding nature trails not only provide gentle introductions to hiking in the Park, they also are excellent ways to learn more about the human and natural history of the Smokies—for instance, how pioneers made their living here, what creatures inhabit a spruce-fir forest, and how a forest recovers from logging operations. Brochures keyed to stops along these trails are available for nominal fees at the trailheads and at book sales areas in the visitor centers. Nature trails are located throughout the Park.

Many of the pullouts on Park roads feature what are called wayside exhibits. These signs, complete with graphics and text, describe a specific aspect of interest at that point. They are worth taking the time to read and are a quick way to absorb some of the fascinating facts about the Smokies.

During your sojourn in the Smokies you may wish to have with you a traveling companion—a book entitled *Mountain Roads & Quiet Places*. Its premise is that "Things worth seeing are worth knowing." There is a story about this place that is worth hearing. Throughout the Park there are numbered signposts along the roads, each color-coded and numbered to correspond with the text in the book. As you explore and read, you will enrich your visit to the Smokies immeasurably. The book may be purchased at book sales areas in the visitor centers.

One other source of information awaits you, and is as close as your radio dial. Tune in to frequency 1610 AM wherever you see signs to do so in the Park. A recorded message provides information about the area you are entering.

For a more intensive learning experience in the Smokies, you may wish to investigate the Great Smoky Mountains Institute at Tremont. I joined teacher/naturalist Paula Bowers and a group of Knox County, Tennessee, fifth graders at the Institute on a drizzly autumn morning. It was the first day of a five-day stay for the students who would spend the morning on a series of quests in the forest.

The instructions were to smell, taste, listen, and feel the environment. In neon orange, yellow, pink, lavender, and red raincoats as bright as the autumn leaves, we tromped up the Falls Trail. There were a few sighs and groans as we hit the steep part, but one young man allowed that this was more fun than recess.

With clipboards and paper, each student was stationed in the woods for a "solo." They were to sit quietly and record observations about themselves and their relationship to nature. This was pretty heady

The Park's Junior Ranger program deputizes children ages 8-12. HOWARD KELLEY.

LITTLE GREENBRIER SCHOOL

Miss Elsie Burrell loves children and loves to teach. It shows in her smile as she stands before a classroom full of youngsters at the Little Greenbrier School. Miss Elsie regularly meets with children at the historic school on the northern edge of Great Smoky Mountains National Park. An educator for twenty-seven years, she now dons a calico bonnet and volunteers her time, sharing recollections of what school was like at Little Greenbrier before the area became a national park.

The school year was short in those days. Children attended for six to eight weeks, then went back home to work in the fields. Education consisted of the basics—reading, writing, and arithmetic. A single copy of Webster's *Blue-Back Speller* had to be shared by all the children in one family. Students in grades one through eight met in the one-room school, where they sat on hard wooden benches and did their arithmetic on slates with small, brittle pencils. Erasers were often nothing more than a sleeve. Lunch, said Miss Elsie, was brought in an oak basket or a tin lard bucket, and usually consisted of leftover biscuits, sweet potatoes, and roastin' ears.

Little Greenbrier School, built of yellow-poplar logs in 1882, was used until 1936. It is a mile from Metcalf Bottoms off the Little River Road. Today students walk that mile to and from, to better appreciate what their predecessors did. While there, Miss Elsie engages the visiting scholars in spelling bees, takes them on walks, and breathes life into history.

Historic one-room schools at Cataloochee and near Metcalf Bottoms picnic area continue to educate visitors today. HOWARD KELLEY.

The Smokies' annual Wildflower Pilgrimage draws flower lovers from around the country. JOHN NETHERTON.

stuff for some; twenty minutes without talking to their teacher or fellow students was no small task. But even on the first day, the students were quickly adapting to their outdoor classroom.

There are indeed many ways to learn. The emphasis of the Smoky Mountains Institute is on nature awareness and instilling an environmental ethic. In existence since 1969, the Institute serves elementary and high school students through school programs and summer camp experiences. There are adult programs as well—including teacher and naturalist training, photography and craft workshops, and Elderhostels. The Institute is open year-round, with a resident staff of teacher/naturalists, and is operated by the Great Smoky Mountains Natural History Association. For information about specific events, contact Great Smoky Mountains Institute at Tremont, Great Smoky Mountains National Park, Townsend, Tennessee 37882, Telephone (615) 448-6709.

Another learning opportunity in the Park is the Smoky Mountain Field School, which works in cooperation with the University of Tennessee and Great Smoky Mountains National Park. The Field School's courses are one- to five-day sessions in the Park, supplemented with classroom study. Course selection includes winter botany, animal life, forests and trees, spiders, and mosses, among many. Overnight hikes and winter camping are also offered. For a schedule of the year's activities, contact Smoky Mountain Field School, 2016 Lake Avenue, University of Tennessee, Knoxville, Tennessee 37996-3515.

A big event in the Park each year is the Spring Wildflower Pilgrimage, three days of wildflower walks, motorcades, and photographic tours. The pilgrimage is normally held the last weekend of April when wildflowers are at their peak. Registration is conducted each day of the pilgrimage. There is no advance registration. For additional information write Great Smoky Mountains National Park, Gatlinburg, Tennessee 37738, Telephone (615) 436-1200.

historic buildings

"Were the people really that small or did they just bump their heads a lot?" A man posed this question to a ranger after ducking through the doorways of a few of the old houses in the Smokies.

It's a good question. As the ranger explained, the pioneers weren't especially short in stature. They were simply obeying the laws of necessity. Small doors and windows meant a stronger structure and less heat lost to the outside, an important consideration in buildings whose only central heating was the big stone fireplace at one end of a room.

The visitor had begun to "people" the empty structures. He had noticed how form followed function, and had gained some insight into how early settlers solved problems when they began to build in this new, strange land. The buildings were constructed in direct response to the environment and display a unique architectural, blend of the German, British, and Scotch-Irish heritage of the settlers.

According to Park historian Ed Trout, Great Smoky Mountains National Park has one of the best collections of log buildings in the eastern United

The Park features one of the most impressive collections of historic log buildings found anywhere (left). HOWARD KELLEY.

Elsie Burrell teaches the old ways at the Little Greenbrier School (above).
HOWARD KELLEY.

BEEGUMS

In the mountains a "feller was considered trifling" if he didn't have a dozen or so beegums.

These hives, like the ones at the Pioneer Farmstead at Oconaluftee, were simple affairs. A two- or three-foot section of hollow black gum was set on a wooden platform, with a board and rock on top to keep out the rain.

A swarm of honeybees was captured and toted back in a tow sack, to be installed in the hive. Beekeepers back then didn't bother with nice frames and foundations and "supers." Two sticks were arranged at right angles and placed midway in the gum, from which the bees could suspend the comb. At harvest time, that stick foundation was removed and the honey and comb cut off. The bees went about their business at will, entering and leaving the hive through neat triangular openings in the base of the gum.

It seemed to work. One farmer got almost 250 pounds of honey one year from thirty beegums, and the sweet liquid fetched ten cents a pound, good money in those days. Besides the income, mountain people believed that watching bees working or swarming brought good luck.

The incredible variety of wildflowers that bloom through spring, summer, and fall provided untold amounts of pollen and nectar. The delicate honey derived from the blossoms of the sourwood tree was considered—and still is for that matter—the best nature can offer, "larrupin good," as they say.

States. Nearly eighty historic structures—houses, barns, outbuildings, churches, schools, and grist mills—have been preserved or rehabilitated in the Park. The best places to see them are at Cades Cove, Cataloochee, Oconaluftee, and along the Roaring Fork Motor Nature Trail. Self-guiding auto tour booklets are available at each place to enhance your visit.

The buildings evoke a strong sense of the past. As you step inside an old home the rich odor of woodsmoke and apples carries you back to a time, not all that long ago, when people, as one author put it, "pressed close to the breast of the earth and danced with the seasons far more than we."

Many of the log buildings in the Smokies represent a common means of construction throughout nineteenth-century, frontier America. Logs were hewed from trees, the material most readily available. In the Smoky Mountains, yellow-poplar was a favorite, along with the now-vanished chestnut.

If winter were pressing and a family needed shelter in a hurry, the logs were left round, the ends jagged. At the first chance, though, this rude structure would be recycled as an outbuilding and a better cabin would be built. For this—the classic Appalachian log cabin—logs were scored along their length, hewn with a broad axe, and possibly smoothed with an adze and even hand planed. Spaces, or chinks, between the logs were filled with mud and mortar. Sometimes logs were split and matched, one log on one side of the house, the match on the other side, a technique that John Davis used in his fine house which now stands at the Oconaluftee Farmstead.

Cabins were usually rectangular, with one large room, although a rear shed, kitchen, and additional living space were added as time and circumstance allowed. The "dog-trot" style was common, with a central breezeway and a main room on each side. The "saddle-bag" house, like the Alfred Reagan home in Roaring Fork, has two halves arranged around a central chimney. The Reagan house, incidentally, was later improved with a style of construction to which most people probably aspired. It was weatherboarded with sawn boards and paneling, and painted white with turquoise trim, the only colors Sears & Roebuck offered at the time.

Corners of log cabins were usually notched and the logs joined without benefit of nails or screws. Not surprisingly, the precision of the notches indicated the craftsmanship of the builder. Half dovetail notches, with flat bottoms and angled tops, were the type almost universally used in the Southern Appalachians. Again, these notches had a function. The outward-sloping top of the notch channeled water out so it would not remain and rot the wood.

Chimneys were attached to the outside of the house. Field stones, in great supply, were sledded in and mortared in place. Occasionally brick was used for a chimney, with fine examples to be seen at the Henry Whitehead and Dan Lawson houses in Cades Cove. Roofs were shingled with split oak, a time-consuming task then (and now). The roof on the barn at the Oconaluftee Farmstead requires 16,000 handsplit oak shingles!

The barn at the Cable Mill area in Cades Cove is a study in engineering genius. Two main weighted beams, each about thirty-five feet long, support the structure in what is called cantilever construction. An

overhang kept animals and farm equipment out of the elements.

Location of houses and barns and outbuildings was not accidental. Their backs faced the prevailing winds, and smokehouses were often near the kitchen. The ever-important springhouse, a simple wooden or rock building which covered a spring, protected the water from contamination by animals and cooled the milk, cheese, and butter.

Great pride was taken in building churches, like the Palmer Chapel in Cataloochee and the Primitive Baptist Church at Cades Cove. Though simple, they were often weatherboarded and kept spanking clean with whitewash.

Two schools can be seen in the Park as well, including Little Greenbrier School near Metcalf Bottoms off the Little River Road, which dates to 1882, and the turn-of-the-century Beech Grove School in Cataloochee. 🍁

Some log structures were built without using a single nail or screw (left). HOWARD KELLEY.

The Park's most impressive collections of historic buildings can be found at Cades Cove, Cataloochee, Oconaluftee, and Roaring Fork (right). KEN L. JENKINS.

Over 100,000 acres of virgin forest thrive in the Smokies (left). HOWARD KELLEY.

forests

From the Carlos Campbell overlook you can see seven distinct forest types (right). JOHN NETHERTON.

The Smokies' spruce-fir forests are rare, island-like ecosystems, having more in common with the boreal forest of Canada than the hardwood forests which surround them (far right). JOHN NETHERTON.

Trees. Everywhere you look there are trees in the Smoky Mountains—more than a hundred species, a diversity unknown almost anywhere else in the world. The forest was the reason that Great Smoky Mountains National Park was created.

By the 1920s logging in what is now the National Park had reached a fever pitch. Large-scale operations, with attendant rail lines, sawmills, boom towns, and forest fires, were taking out millions of board feet of lumber. What seems almost unimaginable today as we look out over the extensive forest is the fact that almost two-thirds of the pre-Park land was completely logged.

The shocking effects impressed Park advocate Horace Kephart and others with the urgency of saving the primeval forest that was left and letting the ravaged land restore itself. The tremendous task to create the national park involved purchasing more than 6,600 parcels of private land, 85 percent of which belonged to the timber companies. But it was done, and in 1934 Great Smoky Mountains National Park was established.

Within its 500,000 acres are found some eight forest types nurtured by sixty to eighty inches of precipitation a year. The full range of types is best seen from the Carlos Campbell Overlook on the Newfound Gap Road, a few miles from Sugarlands. At the lowest elevations are the yellow-poplar and oak-maple community, then mixed oak, pine-oak on drier slopes, cove hardwoods, eastern hemlock, northern hardwoods of yellow birch and American beech, grass and heath balds, and spruce-fir forests at the highest elevations in the eastern part of the Park.

One of the miracles of the Smokies are the virgin forests, trees that have never felt the logger's ax or saw. Good places to see these magnificent trees are in the Albright Grove on the way to Cosby, on the Ramsay Cascade Trail, above Laurel Falls, at the upper end of Noland Divide Trail, and up Bradley Fork from Smokemont; the hemlocks on the Grotto Falls Trail and the spruce-fir forests anywhere along the Appalachian Trail are also fine examples. Tucked in remote locations in the mountains are record-breaking champions—a yellow buckeye, a red hickory, a Fraser magnolia, a Carolina silverbell, and a red spruce— each more than a hunderd feet tall and twelve to eighteen feet in circumference.

The Smoky Mountains have been called a cradle of vegetation, where during ice-age times both conifers and deciduous trees found refuge from the cold. After the glaciers receded, the conifers moved to the highest slopes while the deciduous trees spread over the eastern United States. ❧

SPRUCE-FIR FOREST

Up on Clingmans Dome, Mount LeConte, or any of the other high peaks on the east side of the Great Smokies, you will be in the midst of the shady, evergreen coolness of the spruce-fir forest. These trees of the north woods of Maine and Canada are of great botanic interest, for here they reach the southern limits of their range and form isolated islands of vegetation.

Along the Spruce-Fir Nature Trail you are introduced to the unique character of this community—the sweet smell of the resinous needles and cones and bark, the spongy moss at their feet, shamrock-leaved wood sorrel, and the witch hobble shrub. Red crossbills, red-breasted nuthatches, and red squirrels munch the seeds from the spruce cones. Dark-eyed juncos, black-capped chickadees, and ravens lend voice to the woods.

But the forest is in trouble. Ghostly gray skeletons of Fraser fir tell of a deadly threat to these trees. An aphidlike insect, the balsam woolly adelgid, attaches to the bark of the fir, feeding on the sap and injecting toxin from its saliva. The tree will die in three to seven years.

The adelgid is a non-native insect introduced in this country around 1900 and first found in the Smokies in 1963. In 1982 the Park Service began spraying a soapy solution on accessible fir trees to eliminate the insect. Hope rests in research that may develop both a resistant strain of fir trees and an insecticide that could be more widely applied.

OPPORTUNITIES

70

Visitors to the Smokies are drawn to waterfalls like bears to honey (far left). HOWARD KELLEY.

Waterfalls play a music few people ever tire of (left). JOHN NETHERTON.

Waterfalls like this one appear after a drenching rain and may vanish by the time the sun comes out (right). JOHN NETHERTON.

Grotto Falls, off Roaring Fork Motor Nature Trail, is a favorite destination for dayhikers (far right). JOHN NETHERTON.

"If there is magic

on this planet,

it is contained in water."

—Loren Eiseley

waterfalls

There is an undeniable magic in water, as the late Loren Eiseley so eloquently observed, and waterfalls seem to work that magic in a most superlative way.

Waterfalls move with force and purpose, not like the serendipitous, yielding flow of streams. Their youthful exuberance contrasts mightily with the great age of these mountains. They exist where water has worn away softer rock faster than harder rock. The resistant hard rock forms cliffs, over which the water cascades, either in huge volumes or in silky threads. To come upon one, hidden deep up a ravine in the Smoky Mountains, is to feel like the first discoverer.

Besides their aesthetic value, waterfalls are fine places to find salamanders. Though usually out on rainy nights, salamanders have been seen in broad daylight. Veteran Smokies hiker Carson Brewer reported a "conference of salamanders" at Henwallow Falls, a sight he has never witnessed again. Some twenty-three species of salamanders live in the Park, a diversity nearly unequaled. They come in marbled and spotted, four-toed and black-chinned, long-tailed and three-lined. The red-cheeked salamander is of great

WATERFALLS

Here's a list of waterfalls along trails, with trailhead location and round-trip mileages of the walks:

Rainbow Falls
(Cherokee Orchard Road, 5½ miles)

Grotto Falls
(Roaring Fork Motor Nature Trail, 3 miles)

Ramsay Cascades
(Greenbrier Cove, 8 miles)

Henwallow Falls
(Cosby Campground, 4 miles)

Indian Creek Falls
(Deep Creek Campground, 2 miles)

Juneywhank Falls
(Deep Creek Campground, 1½ miles)

Tom's Branch Falls
(Deep Creek Campground, ½ mile)

Abrams Falls
(Cades Cove Loop Road, 5 miles)

Laurel Falls
(Laurel Falls Parking Area, Little River Road, 2½ miles)

interest because it is found nowhere else in the world but in these mountains. The hellbender is one you wouldn't want to meet in a dark alley—females attain lengths of over two feet.

But if you're looking only for waterfalls, you'll no doubt want to know where they are. Three of the dozen or so in the Park are along roads, while others require walks of varying distances along everything from a short, paved trail to a strenuous, all-day hike.

The Sinks and Meigs Falls can be seen along the Little River Road on the way to Cades Cove. Many years ago I received firsthand contact with The Sinks on a day in February. I skipped down the bank to get a closer look at the frothing mass and without missing a beat slid right into the stream. It was a heart-stopping experience that I care never to repeat. The third waterfall near a road is one with the descriptive name Place of a Thousand Drips, which intermittently streams over the rocks beside the Roaring Fork Motor Nature Trail.

the balds

The Smokies' unusual grassy balds are home to many rare and threatened plants (left). HOWARD KELLEY.

Balds provide panoramic views and an openness not found elsewhere in the Park (right). HOWARD KELLEY.

Balds are curious things. They are treeless areas in mountains where there is no treeline, like "pieces of prairie lifted thousands of feet into the air," wrote naturalist Edwin Way Teale.

How they came to exist in the Southern Appalachians is something of a mystery. Biologists have speculated that ice storms, insects, grazing, blowdowns, woolly mammoths, dry winds, fire, or Indian occupation might explain their origins. Others refer to a Cherokee legend: Pleased with the people for slaying a monster, the Great Spirit willed that the highest mountains should be destitute of trees so enemies could always be seen.

Balds are unique in these mountains, rich in plants and animals that cannot live in the forests. Hawks soar over them, hunting for mice and shrews. One hundred seventy-five species of plants have been identified on Gregory Bald alone, among them some rare and endangered species. And balds are beautiful places to be. Their openness permits uplifting views of the surrounding mountains, in stark contrast to the closed forest.

There are grassy balds and heath balds, an important distinction in discussing causes and management. Heath balds, or "slicks," consist of shrubs like rhododendron and mountain laurel, and they appear to be stable communities. Grass balds, now predominantly mountain oat grass, appear to be closing in with trees. About twenty grassy balds have been identified in Great Smoky Mountains National Park, at an average elevation of 5,100 feet. Some biologists predict that if natural succession continues all will be gone in thirty to seventy years.

In light of their values, the National Park Service has decided to manage some grassy balds in the condition they appeared when the Park was established in 1934. Andrews and Gregory balds are being maintained by cutting back trees as they grow in.

Balds need to be seen to be appreciated. Andrews Bald, at 5,860 feet, is the highest and closest grassy bald, only a two-mile walk on the Forney Ridge Trail from the Clingmans Dome parking area. After a wrong turn caused by my own carelessness, and two extra miles later, I arrived at Andrews Bald one morning. Fog obscured the view, but the place was deserted and I was happy to be there. The golden grasses were soaked in mist, and a few shrubs had sprung up in the meadow. I perched on a rock and soaked in the view of the immediate foothills, the ridges occasionally lit by shafts of sunlight. The darkness and claustrophobia of the forests was behind me; with such a domain within my purview, I imagined how a golden eagle must feel sometimes.

Silers Bald is also accessible from Clingmans Dome, four miles west on the Appalachian Trail. Gregory Bald may be approached from the Parson Branch Road, and in early summer hikers and botanists come from all over the country to see its display of flame azaleas. Other grassy balds include Spence Field, Russell Field, Little Bald, and Thunderhead, all along the Appalachian Trail above the Cades Cove area.

For an interesting comparison, hike to a heath

bald, like the one on top of Brushy Mountain, accessible from Greenbrier or Grotto Falls. This and other balds, with no obscuring trees, provide splendid vistas of the Smoky Mountains. ❦

During early summer, balds sport beautiful displays of rhododendron, flame azalea, and other flowers (left). HOWARD KELLEY.

Gregory Bald is unique for its proliferation of flame azalea hybrids (right).
NATIONAL PARK SERVICE.

bears & other wildlife

A mother bear will often send her cubs up a tree when she feels they are threatened (left).
KEN L. JENKINS.

The Park is one of the few places left in the East where you still stand a chance to glimpse a bear in a wilderness setting (right). KEN L. JENKINS.

You never know when you're going to see a bear in the Smokies.

It was a quiet summer afternoon in Cosby Campground. I was sitting at my campsite reading when I heard a commotion behind me. The branches of a tall hemlock were rustling, and I quickly found the cause. A young black bear had clawed and muscled its way up that tree in seconds. I was impressed.

In a few minutes the bear hustled down the tree and lumbered toward my campsite. It stopped and sniffed the air, sensing humans perhaps. Though I wanted to watch it, I sought some degree of shelter behind the car door. I felt silly, but knew it was wise to keep my distance.

The bear ignored me, snuffling in the leaves in the creekbed for food. The message, for me, was that bear sightings are unpredictable privileges. Visitors may have their best chance of seeing a bear in Cades Cove, but beyond that these animals can appear anywhere anytime in the Smokies.

All winter that bear had been in a den, likely in the hollow of a standing tree. Cubs are born and are nursed during this time. In spring bears emerge from their semi-hibernation, hungry and ready to eat what early grasses, squawroot, and beetles they can find. In summer the berry harvest is theirs, and they will breed, possibly in June. By late summer and early fall they are engaged in a feeding frenzy, building up fat reserves to get them through the winter. Bears will eat nearly anything they can find, although nuts and acorns are favored at this time of year.

Biologists estimate there are 400 to 600 black bears in the Smoky Mountains. Progress has been made over the years to lessen bad encounters between people and bears. Roadside "panhandling" bears have been removed to the backcountry, and Park visitors have begun to exercise more care in keeping their food from bears. Poaching remains a serious problem in the Park. The bears are taken illegally for nothing more than their paws and gall bladders, which are of great value in the Orient.

Though the bears are the real traffic stoppers in the Smokies, wildlife enthusiasts have much more here to delight them. The large, undivided land mass of the Smokies and the several habitat types make it a sanctuary for a diverse number of animals. Some fifty species of mammals, two hundred kinds of birds, twenty-three species of snakes, twenty-three salamander species, and seventy species of fish live here.

You will likely see white-tailed deer, which have made a comeback since the Park was established. A red squirrel, or "boomer," may scold you as you pass through its territory. Woodchucks, mice, skunks, cottontail rabbits, and various other furry creatures are also about. And if you head out on a rainy summer night with a red covering over your flashlight, you might find salamanders under logs and rocks.

Your best chances of seeing animals are at dawn or dusk. Open areas, like the meadows of Cataloochee and Cades Cove, are especially good places to see wildlife. Bring binoculars and patience, and move slowly and quietly. 🍁

Logging and over-hunting had all but eliminated deer from the Smokies prior to Park establishment (above). KEN L. JENKINS.

It's not uncommon to see a raccoon or two in Cades Cove (left). KEN L. JENKINS.

OPPORTUNITIES
76

Of the 23 species of snakes found in the Park, only the copperhead (shown) and timber rattlesnake are poisonous (above).
NATIONAL PARK SERVICE.

Rapid weather changes can be trouble for hikers (right). JOHN NETHERTON.

safety

Okay, let's admit it. Safety isn't very sexy. The only thing that seems to garner big headlines is when an accident happens. When somebody gets hurt. Suddenly, the vacation is ruined.

Be safe, not sorry. The rules and the signs in the Park exist for a reason. Don't climb on waterfalls. The algae and moss that grow on the rocks are as slippery as a coating of ice. Climbing on the rockfaces at Clingmans Dome and Newfound Gap is also ill advised, especially for children.

Hypothermia or "exposure," discussed more fully in the backcountry hiking section of this book, is not just a winter threat. Be prepared for rapid weather changes in these mountains at any time of year. A hat and gloves, a windbreaker, dry clothes, and high-energy foods and plenty of fluids will go a long way in preventing hypothermia. Know the symptoms and the treatment.

DON'T FEED THE BEARS. Period. This warning deserves capital letters because it seems to be the rule most often ignored. Bears are wild animals, perfectly able to obtain food from their environment. When a handful of potato chips is extended, they may understandably believe that the arm attached is also being offered for their consumption. Keep your campsite clean, and pack all food, cooking utensils, and ice chests out of sight in your vehicle. In the backcountry, sling your food bag on a line stretched between two trees, at least ten feet off the ground and four feet from the nearest limb or trunk. Also don't attempt to pet, tease, molest, or otherwise approach a bear. They are unpredictable animals.

There are two poisonous snakes in the Smokies, copperheads and timber rattlesnakes. Snakebites are not a major cause of injury, but you should be careful stepping over logs or rocks and poking around old buildings. These snakes are also fond of sunning in the openings in pine-oak forests. If you are bitten, seek medical attention immediately.

Yellowjackets can be a problem in July, August, and September. Stay clear of them, watch where you sit, and you may wish to remove rings before you hike because of swelling caused by stings. If you know you are severely allergic to insect stings, include an anaphylaxis kit in your pack or glove compartment.

Poison ivy is common below 3,000 feet elevation, especially along fences, roads, and streams. Learn its characteristic three-part leaf and avoid it.

Ticks—common in grassy, shrubby, and wooded areas—have become more of a problem to outdoor users lately. They transmit not only Rocky Mountain spotted fever but also an illness called Lyme disease. To avoid tick bites, tuck in your pants legs and shirt, wear repellant, and inspect your head and body for ticks. If bitten, remove the tick by grasping it with tweezers and gently pulling it out. If the tick mouth-parts remain in the skin, get medical attention.

the seasons

In the Smoky Mountains in spring, there must be as many words for green as the Eskimos have for snow. The new leaves on the trees are every shade imaginable—chartreuse, lime, emerald, olive, and aquamarine. Redbud and dogwood spatter the hills with pink and white. (Old-timers warn that when the dogwood trees bloom, you can look for a cold spell known as "dogwood winter.")

Arthur Stupka, who served as Park naturalist in the Great Smokies for twenty-five years, made remarkable records of seasonal happenings in the Park.

We are indebted to him for his careful observations, many of which are included here.

In keeping with the tradition Mr. Stupka set, Park naturalists still file a "Blooming Report" to chart the progress of the flowering plants that grow here. On almost any trail in the Park you can see some of the more than one thousand species of wildflowers that bloom in the Smokies. Anemone, bellflower, bishop's cap, bloodroot, chickweed, cinquefoil, phacelia, toothwort, trillium, trout lily, and violets appear in early April. By mid-month bleeding hearts, bluets,

All four seasons in the Smokies are filled with wonders and surprises (left).
KEN L. JENKINS.

May ushers in mountain laurel, blooming up and down the mountains (right).
JOHN NETHERTON.

OPPORTUNITIES

78

LEAF COLOR

We all learned in elementary school that leaves are green because they contain chlorophyll. We probably also learned that it was Old Jack Frost who turned them gold and red in autumn. Well, the story has changed a bit.

Those who have studied the biology of leaf colors now tell us that in the days of autumn those green pigments dwindle. They have been "masking" other pigments that have been in the leaf all along — the carotenoids which give yellow, brown, and orange, the same pigments that give carrots their color.

It's a little different with the reds and purples. They belong to a group called anthocyanins, the same pigments that make apples red and grapes purple. These colors develop late in the summer in the sap of the leaf cells as sugar breaks down in bright light. The brighter the light, the more anthocyanins, and thus the brighter the reds and purples and their combinations. But Nature, in her infinite variety, doesn't let one kind of leaf have the carotenoids and another the anthocyanins. Both types can occur in the same leaf, giving all possible hues.

It isn't frost so much as sunny, clear, warm days, combined with a drop in temperature at night, that will produce the finest colors. And in a year when that combination occurs, there is no place better in the world to be than in Great Smoky Mountains National Park.

buttercups, Dutchman's breeches, fire pinks, fringed polygala, hawkweed, iris, mayapple, Solomon's seal, and vetch are added to the list. By May, blue-eyed grass, columbine, coralroot, foamflower, lady's slipper, squawroot, and speedwell have joined.

In June and July flame azaleas, mountain laurel, and Catawba rhododendron spangle the high balds. Berry season arrives—wild strawberries, blackberries, dewberries, and gooseberries—and with them the black bears, in a feeding frenzy.

Henry David Thoreau asked, "Do not the flowers of August and September generally resemble suns and stars—sunflowers and asters and the single flowers of the goldenrod?" In August tall, leggy flowers stretch for sunlight through the heavy leaf canopy, fed by the month's heavy rains. Turk's cap lily, ironweed, cardinal flower, jewelweed, and turtlehead line roads and streams.

The squirrels know something we don't, though. They are already harvesting hickory nuts, for by September the first frost will have browned the ferns. The fruits of fall begin to ripen, and the appearance of winter birds like the white-throated sparrow and ruby-crowned kinglet is noted.

By October the mountains are ready once again to put on a show comparable to spring's wildflower extravaganza. It is fall color time, an event of such notoriety that headlines of area newspapers report the status of the turning: "Mountains Beginning Fall Show," "Autumn's Colors Still Have Not Peaked," "Autumn Colors Arrive Early," and "Colors Remain Strong."

Depending on who you ask about the "peak," you'll learn that a good rain is all that's needed. Someone else says no, we only need more of the same—cold nights and warm, sunny days. In truth, the peaks occur at different places and different times. From about October 15 through 31 the colors march up the hillsides—the reds of sourwood and sumac, yellows of hickory and birch, browns of oak, and the splendid scarlet of the sugar maples.

You may hike nearly any trail in the Park to see the flames of autumn, smell the richness of the leaves, and crunch them underfoot. If you choose to drive, favorite color "hot spots" include Lakeshore Drive from Bryson City to Noland Creek, the Blue Ridge Parkway, Balsam Mountain Road from Heintooga Picnic Area to Round Bottom, the Gatlinburg Bypass, western side of the Foothills Parkway, and Rich Mountain Road off the Cades Cove loop.

You might also watch for monarch butterflies, fluttering like falling leaves as they begin their long journey south to their wintering ground in Mexico. To predict the force and timing of winter, mountain folk mark the departure of hummingbirds and arrival of hermit thrushes, the location of hornets' nests, and the thickness of spider webs. If the hornets build nests close to the ground and the spider webs are thick, winter will be early and cold.

The short days of Indian summer signal the deciduous trees to drop their leaves so they can withstand winter drought. Rather than a time of death, winter is a time of rest, for plants and animals alike. A time when the land can restore itself. Snow can fall in the high country of the Smokies as early as October, though it is more common in the next few

OPPORTUNITIES

79

months. The earliest snowfall on record was at Newfound Gap on September 26, 1949. Whenever it happens, people from farther south flock to see what for them is a rare sight.

Some roads in the Park are closed all winter, especially secondary and gravel roads and the road to Clingmans Dome. After a snowfall, tire chains may be required on some sections. To obtain current information on weather conditions in Tennessee call (615) 436-1200, and in North Carolina (704) 497-9146. 🍁

When the fall colors will peak is always a hot topic of discussion, but from mid-October to mid-November there will be a lot of autumn splendor to be enjoyed (left). JOHN NETHERTON.

Winter weather is extremely variable, ranging from balmy warm fronts with highs in the 60s to cold snaps with biting lows of minus 20 (right). JOHN NETHERTON.

You can do a lot of learning about the Smokies even between trips (left).

KEN L. JENKINS.

The people of the Southern Appalachians have a rich, beautiful culture you could spend years exploring (right). HOWARD KELLEY.

suggested readings

Delaughter, Jerry. *Mountain Roads & Quiet Places.* A Complete Guide to the Roads of Great Smoky Mountains National Park. Great Smoky Mountains Natural History Association, Gatlinburg. 1986.

Doolittle Jerome. *The Southern Appalachians.* Time-Life Books, New York. 1975.

Dykeman, Wilma and Jim Stokely. *At Home in the Smokies.* Handbook 125. National Park Service, Washington, D.C. 1984.

Fisher, Ronald M. *The Appalachian Trail.* National Geographic Society, Washington, D.C. 1972.

Frome, Michael. *Strangers in High Places.* University of Tennessee Press, Knoxville. Revised edition, 1980.

Johnsson, Robert G. Illustrated by John Dawson. *A Naturalist's Notebook.* Great Smoky Mountains Natural History Association, Gatlinburg. 1984.

Kephart, Horace. *Our Southern Highlanders.* University of Tennessee Press, Knoxville. 1984.

Kirk, Don. *Smoky Mountains Trout Fishing Guide.* Menasha Ridge Press, Birmingham. Revised edition, 1985.

Murlless, Dick and Constance Stallings. *Hiker's Guide to the Smokies.* Sierra Club Books, San Francisco. 1973.

Netherton, John and David Duhl. *A Guide to Photography and the Smoky Mountains.* Cumberland Valley Press, Nashville. 1988.

Powers, Elizabeth with Mark Hannah. *Cataloochee. Lost Settlement of the Smokies.* Powers-Hannah Publications, Charleston, SC. 1982.

Shelton, Napier. *Great Smoky Mountains.* Handbook 112. National Park Service, Washington, D.C. 1981.

Shields, Randolph. *The Cades Cove Story.* Great Smoky Mountains Natural History Association, Gatlinburg. 1977.